12/08

W9-BRS-369

3 2186 00174 6147

Diagnosis and Treatment of Cancer

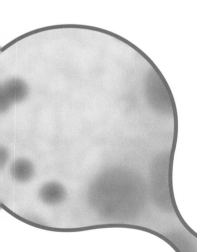

Diagnosis and Treatment of Cancer

Lyman Lyons

Consulting Editor,
Donna M. Bozzone, Ph.D.
Professor of Biology
Saint Michael's College

CHELSEA HOUSE
PUBLISHERS
An imprint of Infobase Publishing

Fossil Ridge Public Library District
Braidwood, IL 60408

THE BIOLOGY OF CANCER: DIAGNOSIS AND TREATMENT OF CANCER

Copyright @ 2007 by Infobase Publishing, Inc.

All rights reserved. No part of this book may be reproduced or utilized in any form or by any means, electronic or mechanical, including photocopying, recording, or by any information storage or retrieval systems, without permission in writing from the publisher. For information, contact:

Chelsea House
An imprint of Infobase Publishing
132 West 31st Street
New York NY 10001

Library of Congress Cataloging-in-Publication Data
Lyons, Lyman.
  Diagnosis and treatment of cancer / Lyman Lyons.
      p. ; cm.— (The Biology of cancer)
  Includes bibliographical references and index.
  ISBN-13: 978-0-7910-8826-5
  ISBN-10: 0-7910-8826-X
  1. Cancer—Popular works. 2. Cancer—Diagnosis—Popular works. 3. Cancer—Treatment—Popular works. 4. Cancer—Diagnosis. 5. Cancer—Treatment. I. Title. II. Series.
  [DNLM: 1. Neoplasms—diagnosis. 2. Neoplasms—therapy. QZ 241 L991d 2007]

  RC263.L96 2007
  616.99'4—ßdc22   2007009175

Chelsea House books are available at special discounts when purchased in bulk quantities for businesses, associations, institutions, or sales promotions. Please call our Special Sales Department in New York at (212) 967-8800 or (800) 322-8755.

You can find Chelsea House on the World Wide Web at http://www.chelseahouse.com

Text design by James Scotto-Lavino
Cover design by Ben Peterson
Illustrations by Chris and Elisa Scherer

Printed in the United States of America

Bang EJB 10 9 8 7 6 5 4 3 2 1

This book is printed on acid-free paper.

All links and Web addresses were checked and verified to be correct at the time of publication. Because of the dynamic nature of the Web, some addresses and links may have changed since publication and may no longer be valid.

Taxol® is a registered trademark of Bristol-Myers Squibb Company.

CONTENTS

◆

FOREWORD

◆

Approximately 1,500 people die each day of cancer in the United States. Worldwide, more than 8 million new cases are diagnosed each year. In affluent, developed nations such as the United States, around 1 out of 3 people will develop cancer in his or her lifetime. As deaths from infection and malnutrition become less prevalent in developing areas of the world, people live longer and cancer incidence increases to become a leading cause of mortality. Clearly, few people are left untouched by this disease due either to their own illness or that of loved ones. This situation leaves us with many questions: What causes cancer? Can we prevent it? Is there a cure?

Cancer did not originate in the modern world. Evidence of humans afflicted with cancer dates from ancient times. Examinations of bones from skeletons that are more than 3,000 years old reveal structures that appear to be tumors. Records from ancient Egypt, written more than 4,000 years ago, describe breast cancers. Possible cases of bone tumors have been observed in Egyptian mummies that are more than 5,000 years old. It is even possible that our species' ancestors developed cancer. In 1932, Louis Leakey discovered a jawbone, from either *Australopithecus* or *Homo erectus*, that possessed what appeared to be a tumor. Cancer specialists examined the jawbone and suggested that the tumor was due to Burkitt's lymphoma, a type of cancer that affects the immune system.

It is likely that cancer has been a concern for the human lineage for at least a million years.

Human beings have been searching for ways to treat and cure cancer since ancient times, but cancer is becoming an even greater problem today. Because life expectancy increased dramatically in the twentieth century due to public health successes such as improvements in our ability to prevent and fight infectious disease, more people live long enough to develop cancer. Children and young adults can develop cancer, but the chance of developing the disease increases as a person ages. Now that so many people live longer, cancer incidence has increased dramatically in the population. As a consequence, the prevalence of cancer came to the forefront as a public health concern by the middle of the twentieth century. In 1971 President Richard Nixon signed the National Cancer Act and thus declared "war" on cancer. The National Cancer Act brought cancer research to the forefront and provided funding and a mandate to spur research to the National Cancer Institute. During the years since that action, research laboratories have made significant progress toward understanding cancer. Surprisingly, the most dramatic insights came from learning how normal cells function, and by comparing that to what goes wrong in cancer cells.

Many people think of cancer as a single disease, but it actually comprises more than 100 different disorders in normal cell and tissue function. Nevertheless, all cancers have one feature in common: All are diseases of uncontrolled cell division. Under normal circumstances, the body regulates the production of new cells very precisely. In cancer cells, particular defects in deoxyribonucleic acid, or DNA, lead to breakdowns in the cell communication and growth control that are normal in healthy cells. Having escaped these controls, cancer cells can become invasive and spread to other parts of the body. As a consequence, normal tissue and organ functions may be seriously disrupted. Ultimately, cancer can be fatal.

Even though cancer is a serious disease, modern research has provided many reasons to feel hopeful about the future of cancer treatment and prevention. First, scientists have learned a great deal about the specific genes involved in cancer. This information paves the way for improved early detection, such as identifying individuals with a genetic predisposition to cancer and monitoring their health to ensure the earliest possible detection. Second, knowledge of both the specific genes involved in cancer and the proteins made by cancer cells has made it possible to develop very specific and effective treatments for certain cancers. For example, childhood leukemia, once almost certainly fatal, now can be treated successfully in the great majority of cases. Similarly, improved understanding of cancer cell proteins led to the development of new anticancer drugs such as Herceptin, which is used to treat certain types of breast tumors. Third, many cancers are preventable. In fact, it is likely that more than 50 percent of cancers would never occur if people avoided smoking, overexposure to sun, a high-fat diet, and a sedentary lifestyle. People have tremendous power to reduce their chances of developing cancer by making good health and lifestyle decisions. Even if treatments become perfect, prevention is still preferable to avoid the anxiety of a diagnosis and the potential pain of treatment.

The books in *The Biology of Cancer* series reveal information about the causes of the disease; the DNA changes that result in tumor formation; ways to prevent, detect, and treat cancer; and detailed accounts of specific types of cancers that occur in particular tissues or organs. Books in this series describe what happens to cells as they lose growth control and how specific cancers affect the body. *The Biology of Cancer* series also provides insights into the studies undertaken, the research experiments done, and the scientists involved in the development of the present state of knowledge of this disease. In this way, readers get to see beyond "the facts" and understand more about the process of biomedical research. Finally, the books in *The Biology of Cancer* series provide information to help readers make healthy choices that can reduce the risk of cancer.

Cancer research is at a very exciting crossroads, affording scientists the challenge of scientific problem solving as well as the opportunity to engage in work that is likely to directly benefit people's health and well-being. I hope that the books in this series will help readers learn about cancer. Even more, I hope that these books will capture your interest and awaken your curiosity about cancer so that you ask questions for which scientists presently have no answers. Perhaps some of your questions will inspire you to follow your own path of discovery. If so, I look forward to your joining the community of scientists; after all, there is still a lot of work to be done.

Donna M. Bozzone, Ph.D.
Professor of Biology
Saint Michael's College
Colchester, Vermont

1

WHAT IS CANCER?

KEY POINTS

♦ Cancer is the uncontrolled growth of abnormal cells. It begins when a single abnormal cell divides.

♦ Cancer cells are known as "super cells" because they produce their own growth factors and can divide over and over again and grow anywhere in the body.

♦ Age, genetics, and exposure to certain carcinogens, viruses, ultraviolet rays, and radioactive elements each play a part in an individual's risk of developing cancer.

Jonathan is a healthy 40-year-old man, but something has happened to a single cell in one of his kidneys. Normal kidney cells work together to remove excess water and waste products from the blood so that they can be excreted as urine. But this single cell does not look like a normal kidney cell and doesn't act like one. It begins to divide

11

and produce copies of itself over and over without stopping. Over the next few years, it will produce enough cells to form a lump called a **tumor**, which eventually will cause bloody urine and a pain in Jonathan's side that he will notice. If Jonathan reports these symptoms to his doctor early enough, the cancer can be destroyed and Jonathan can be cured. By this time, however, cells from the cancer might have already migrated to other parts of the body through the bloodstream. If this has happened, new cancers can grow and Jonathan may die.

Cancer is the uncontrolled growth of abnormal cells. Cancer is not one disease but a group of about 200 related diseases that strike different parts of the body. One characteristic that all types of cancer share is that they begin with the division of a single abnormal cell, which continues to divide without stopping. The cancer cell divides into two cells, then four cells, then eight cells, and the number of cells continues to double. After the cells have doubled 30 times, which could take anywhere from a year to more than 40 years, a billion cells have built up into a tumor about 0.4 inch (1 cm) in size (Figures 1.1 and 1.2). At this point, the tumor may be detected by the symptoms it causes, felt by touch, or seen on an X-ray. The tumor will continue to grow larger and will eventually kill the person by damaging vital organs unless treated successfully.

Cancer is not a new disease. Historical records show that people suffered from cancer 4,000 years ago in ancient Egypt. Cancer can affect any part of the body (Table 1.1). The most common sites are the lung, breast (in females), **prostate** (in males), and the **colon** and **rectum**. About 1.4 million new cancer cases were diagnosed in the United States in 2005, and about 570,000 people who already had cancer died—one in every four deaths. Although these figures seem grim, the outlook for a person with cancer is much better than it was in the past. In the 1940s, 25

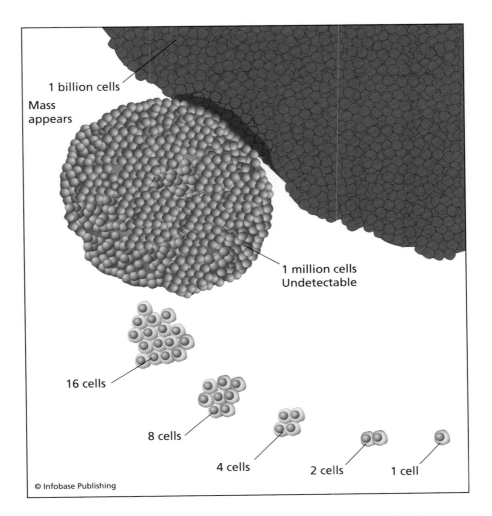

1 billion cells
Mass appears

1 million cells
Undetectable

16 cells

8 cells

4 cells

2 cells

1 cell

© Infobase Publishing

Figure 1.1 A single cancer cell divides into two cells, then four cells, then eight cells, and so on over a period of months or years. Eventually there are enough cells to form a visible tumor.

percent of people with cancer survived five years after being diagnosed. Today, 64 percent survive five years after diagnosis. This improved survival rate is due to earlier detection and better treatments.

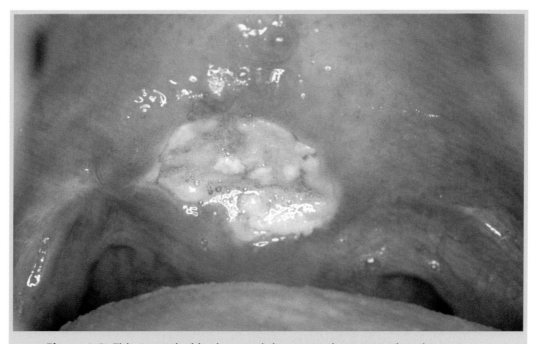

Figure 1.2 This tumor inside the mouth has grown large enough to be seen without special instruments. *(Eamonn McNulty/Photo Researchers, Inc.)*

HOW CANCER CELLS ARE DIFFERENT

Cancer cells look different from normal cells. Normal cells are **differentiated**, or specialized, according to their specific functions in the body. Liver, brain, and lung cells all have a separate function and each type of cell is different in size, shape, and in the specialized processes that occur within it. Cells are organized into tissue, and tissues are further organized into an organ. Cancer cells, on the other hand, are poorly differentiated and do not have a useful function. They do not resemble the nearby normal cells, and they are jumbled together

TABLE 1.1 LEADING SITES OF NEW CANCER CASES AND DEATHS, 2007 ESTIMATES			
ESTIMATED NEW CASES*		**ESTIMATED DEATHS**	
Male	Female	Male	Female
Prostate 218,890 (29%)	Breast 178,480 (26%)	Lung & bronchus 89,510 (31%)	Lung & bronchus 70,880 (26%)
Lung & bronchus 114,760 (15%)	Lung & bronchus 98,620 (15%)	Prostate 27,050 (9%)	Breast 40,460 (15%)
Colon & rectum 79,130 (10%)	Colon & rectum 74,630 (11%)	Colon & rectum 26,000 (9%)	Colon & rectum 26,180 (10%)
Urinary bladder 50,040 (7%)	Uterine corpus 39,080 (6%)	Pancreas 16,840 (6%)	Pancreas 16,530 (6%)
Non-Hodgkin lymphoma 34,200 (4%)	Non-Hodgkin lymphoma 28,990 (4%)	Leukemia 12,320 (4%)	Ovary 15,280 (6%)
Melanoma of the skin 33,910 (4%)	Melanoma of the skin 26,030 (4%)	Liver & intrahepatic bile duct 11,280 (4%)	Leukemia 9,470 (4%)
Kidney & renal pelvis 31,590 (4%)	Thyroid 25,480 (4%)	Esophagus 10,900 (4%)	Non-Hodgkin lymphoma 9,060 (3%)
Leukemia 24,800 (3%)	Ovary 22,430 (3%)	Urinary bladder 9,630 (3%)	Uterine corpus 7,400 (3%)
Oral cavity & pharynx 24,180 (3%)	Kidney & renal pelvis 19,600 (3%)	Non-Hodgkin lymphoma 9,600 (3%)	Brain & other nervous system 5,590 (2%)

(continues)

ESTIMATED NEW CASES*		ESTIMATED DEATHS	
Male	Female	Male	Female
Pancreas 18,830 (2%)	Leukemia 19,440 (3%)	Kidney & renal pelvis 8,080 (3%)	Liver & intrahepatic bile duct 5,500 (2%)
All sites 766,860 (100%)	All sites 678,060 (100%)	All sites 289,550 (100%)	All sites 270,100 (100%)

* Excludes basal and squamous cell skin cancers and in situ carcinoma except urinary bladder.

Note: Percentages may not total 100% due to rounding.
© 2007, American Cancer Society. *Cancer Facts and Figures 2006.* Atlanta: American Cancer Society, Inc.

instead of being organized into tissue. Unlike normal cells, cancer cells vary in size and shape, and the cell **nucleus** is often larger.

A normal cell divides to produce new cells only when it receives a signal from certain **protein** molecules called growth factors that come from outside the cell. Specialized cells produce more than 20 growth factors to control the production of new cells so that the body has the proper number of each type of cell. Growth factors send signals for the cell to divide by attaching themselves to other proteins called growth factor receptors, which are on the surface of the cell. By contrast, a cancer cell can divide without limit because they produce their own growth factors. A cancer cell can also produce growth factor receptors that send signals to other cells to divide even when growth factors are not attached to them.

Normal cells can divide about 50 times before they die because some of the **DNA** at the **telomeres** (tips) of the **chromosomes** (the strands in the cell nucleus that contain genes) is lost with each division. Eventually, these losses damage the chromosomes enough to cause the cell to die. Cancer cells, on the other hand, can divide over and over without stopping because they produce an **enzyme**—a protein that speeds up a chemical reaction—called **telomerase** that replaces the chromosome tips.

If a cell is not needed by the body anymore, or is infected or has damaged DNA, it usually "commits suicide" by a process of programmed cell death called **apoptosis** in which the cell breaks up and is absorbed

---

◆ WHY CELLS MUST DIE

The death of cells in the body is a normal—and necessary—process. To function and stay healthy, the human body produces 50 billion or more new cells a day. About the same number of cells must die each day or the body would quickly bloat up to immense size—and then die.

Consider this: One bacterium can divide into two bacteria in 20 minutes. There would be eight bacteria after one hour, then 64 bacteria after two hours, and so on. If there was unlimited food and no bacteria died, and if the bacteria continued doubling every 20 minutes, there would be 16,777,216 bacteria in eight hours. If the doubling continued for two days, the weight of the bacteria would be much greater than that of the Earth!

On a much smaller scale, this is the problem with cancer cells. In contrast to normal cells, they are not subject to programmed cell death, or apoptosis. They do not die, and if not treated successfully, they continue to divide without limit, damaging vital organs until the body dies.

by other cells. This is a normal process that occurs continuously (see box on page 17). Cancer cells have defects in the apoptosis mechanism and do not commit suicide. They continue to live and divide, producing increasing numbers of cancer cells.

Just like normal cells, cancer cells need the oxygen and nutrients that are supplied by the blood. As the tumor grows to a size of less than 0.1 inch (about 2 millimeters) the cancer cells produce chemical signals that cause blood vessels to grow into the tumor. The normal process of forming new blood vessels, called **angiogenesis**, occurs in a growing embryo and in a wound that is healing. But in cancer, the process ensures that the tumor can continue to grow without starving.

Some tumors are **benign**. They may grow larger, but they stay in one place and can be removed by surgery. Other tumors are **malignant** and are more dangerous: They invade the surrounding tissue and spread to other parts of the body. In order to spread, or **metastasize**, from the original site, a cancer cell breaks away from a tumor and enters a blood vessel or a **lymph node**—a small capsule that contains white blood cells that filter out and destroy bacteria and **viruses**. Once inside a blood vessel or lymph node, the cell is transported to another part of the body. There, the cell divides repeatedly, forms a new tumor, and begins angiogenesis. For example, both kidney cancer and breast cancer can metastasize to the lungs, liver, and bones.

All of these characteristics make cancer cells "super cells." They can grow anywhere in the body and they are immortal: They divide over and over without dying. In 1951, a woman named Henrietta Lacks died from cancer of the **cervix**—the lower part of the uterus. Before her death, doctors removed some of the cancer cells for study. These cells, named

♦ THE MOST FAMOUS CANCER SURVIVOR IN THE WORLD

In 1996, Lance Armstrong was nearing the top in the world of professional bicycle racing at age 25. But in September, his right **testicle** (the male sex organ that produces sperm) became swollen to several times its normal size, and he began to have headaches and cough up blood. Tests showed that he had testicular cancer that had spread to the abdomen, lungs, and brain. Although he was told he had a 50 percent chance of surviving, some doctors privately thought his chances were even lower than that.

Armstrong underwent surgery to remove his testicle and then had another surgery to remove two brain tumors. He began three months of **chemotherapy**—treatments with strong chemicals to kill cancer cells wherever they may be in his body. What followed seems like a miracle. By December 1996 tests showed that his cancer was gone and he resumed training, slowly at first. In 1998 he resumed racing.

In 1999 he astounded the world by winning the Tour de France, an annual race that covers 1,800 to 2,500 miles (2,897 to 4,023 km) in about 20 days. The Tour is the most important bicycle race—and perhaps the most grueling athletic event—in the world. Winning the Tour de France seemed impossible for someone with a body that had been ravaged by cancer and the side effects of chemotherapy just three years earlier. Armstrong followed this victory by winning the Tour de France for seven consecutive years, through 2005—something no other bicycle racer had ever done.

HeLa cells after her, are still alive and dividing in research laboratories around the world, more than 50 years later.

WHAT CAUSES CANCER?

The nucleus of every cell in the human body contains 23 pairs of chromosomes that are made of DNA molecules. Long sections of DNA molecules carry units of information called **genes**. These genes control all the processes in a cell by producing different kinds of proteins (Figure 1.3). When a cell divides, the DNA molecules duplicate themselves, and each new cell receives identical copies of the original genes so that it can continue to function normally.

But sometimes things go wrong. In 1914 German biologist Theodor Boveri proposed the idea that cancer was the result of abnormal chromosomes. The idea that cancer was somehow a genetic disease slowly gathered evidence through the twentieth century. Today we believe that changes in genes, called **mutations**, can convert normal cells into cancer cells. Then, when the cancer cells divide, the mutations in the genes are copied, so more cancer cells are produced. Mutations in perhaps 10 genes out of the 24,000 genes in the human body can cause a cell to become cancerous. These mutations can occur in two kinds of genes: **oncogenes** and **tumor suppressor genes**.

Oncogenes are mutations of normal genes that regulate cell growth and cell division, and can cause cancer cells to divide without stopping. In 1976 Michael Bishop and Harold Varmus of the University of California at San Francisco first isolated an oncogene, named *src*, from a type of chicken cancer. The normal *src* gene produces a protein that passes on signals that control cell growth. When this normal gene mutates (changes) to form the *src* oncogene, it produces a different protein that

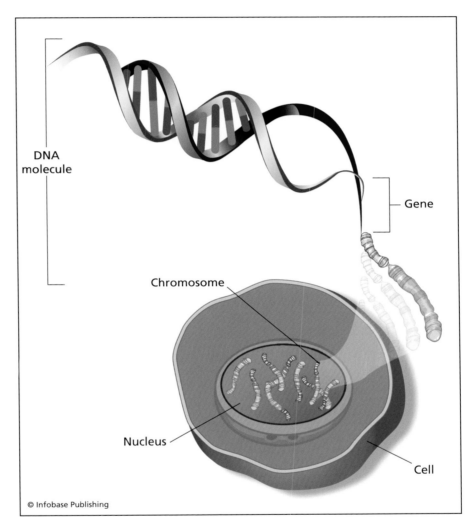

Figure 1.3 The nucleus of every cell in the body contains chromosomes, which are made of DNA molecules. Certain parts of the DNA molecule carry units of information called genes that control all processes in the cell.

sends continual signals for the cell to grow. This protein is found in certain kinds of lung, colon, and breast cancers. More than 100 oncogenes have now been discovered and linked to specific forms of cancer.

Tumor suppressor genes are normal genes that produce proteins to control cell division and prevent cells with damaged DNA from dividing. If these genes are working properly, cells with mutations that could cause them to become cancer cells are prevented from dividing and forming tumors. In 1986 cancer researchers Thaddeus Dryja, Stephen Friend, and Robert Weinberg found the first tumor suppressor gene, *RB*. Mutations of the *RB* gene cause retinoblastoma, a rare cancer of the eye that occurs in infants. In 1989, researchers found the *p53* tumor suppressor gene, which produces a protein that prevents damaged DNA from being copied during cell division and orders the cell to commit suicide by apoptosis. If the *p53* gene mutates and can't function, cancer cells will divide continually, even when their DNA is damaged, and produce a tumor. Mutations in the *p53* gene are found in more than half of all cancers.

WHAT CAUSES GENES TO MUTATE?

Many factors cause mutations in genes that lead to cancer. One factor is easily noticed, even by non-scientists: The incidence of cancer increases with the age of the person. As we age, damage accumulates in the genes in our cells faster than it can be repaired. Some types of damage can cause a cell to become cancerous. About 75 percent of cancers occur in people age 55 or older. For example, about one in 207 women up to age 39 will develop breast cancer, compared to one in 13 at the ages of 60 to 79.

Certain chemicals, known as **carcinogens**, cause mutations that lead to cancer. In 1775 British doctor Percival Pott reported that men who worked as chimney sweeps frequently developed cancer of the scrotum—the sack of skin and muscles holding the testicles. Experiments in 1915 showed that the application of coal tar to the skin of rabbits causes cancer, the first direct experimental evidence that cancers can be caused by external factors. Currently we know of more than 200 carcinogens, including many **organic compounds**, metals, dusts, and combustion products. Carcinogens are found in the workplace and in industrial pollution. For example, asbestos is a mineral made up of fibers, which was used in manufacturing many products such as insulation and roofing materials until it was found to cause lung cancer. Asbestos is still being used in many countries outside North America and Europe. Also chemicals used to produce dyes have been shown to cause bladder cancer.

Not all carcinogens are man-made. Aflatoxin, which causes liver cancer, is a chemical produced by the common fungus *Aspergillu flavus*, which grows on grains stored in warm, moist conditions. The fungus is most common in the tropics.

More than 60 carcinogens are found in tobacco smoke. The incidence of lung cancer rose as cigarette smoking become more common in the twentieth century. In the 1950s experimental evidence linked smoking to cancer. Today we know that the carcinogens from tobacco account for about 30 percent of all cancer deaths and 87 percent of lung cancer deaths. One carcinogen in tobacco smoke is benzopyrene. By itself, benzopyrene does not cause cancer. However, in the liver it is processed into a molecule that attaches itself to DNA in the body's cells. When the cells divide, these attached molecules cause mutations to occur in the copies of DNA in the new cells, sometimes causing them to become cancerous.

Several viruses have been found to cause cancer. A virus is a tiny particle consisting of a DNA or **RNA** core wrapped inside a protein coat. Different viruses infect bacteria, plants, animals, and humans. In humans, they cause diseases such as chicken pox, influenza, and AIDS.

Viruses are so simple, even compared to bacteria, that they are not considered true living organisms. They need living cells to reproduce. A virus enters a cell or injects its DNA or RNA into the cell, and then makes the cell produce copies of the virus. A polio virus can cause 100,000 copies of itself to be produced within a single cell. Certain viruses cause cancer by inserting their DNA into the cell's DNA, or by changing genes in the cell into oncogenes.

In 1911 Peyton Rous of the Rockefeller Institute for Medical Research in New York City discovered that a virus causes cancer in chickens. Since then several other viruses have also been shown to cause cancer. In 1964 a group led by British researchers Michael Anthony Epstein and Yvonne Barr at Middlesex Hospital in London linked a virus directly to human cancer for the first time. The Epstein-Barr virus is common in humans and causes **mononucleosis** (the "kissing disease"), but most of the time its presence does not cause illness. The virus also can cause several rare types of cancers, including Burkitt's lymphoma, which is mostly found in Africa. About one-third of the 670,000 new cases of liver cancers worldwide in 2005 were caused by **hepatitis** B and hepatitis C viruses, which damage the liver even when they don't lead to cancer. Almost 100 percent of women with cancer of the cervix are infected with human papillomavirus, with about 490,000 new cases worldwide in 2005, mostly outside the United States and Europe. Infection with this virus is common in both men and women. Fortunately most infected women do not develop cancer.

Radiation in the form of UV (ultraviolet) radiation from the sun, **radioactive elements**, and X-rays can damage DNA and lead to mutations. When radiation enters a cell, it knocks **electrons** from molecules and creates an ionized molecule—a molecule with an electrical charge. The ionized molecule could be DNA itself or a different molecule in the cell that then reacts with DNA. In either case the radiation produces a mutation in DNA.

Exposure to ultraviolet radiation from the sun or tanning beds significantly increases the risk of developing **melanoma**, the most serious type of skin cancer, which accounts for about 4 percent of all cancers. People are exposed to radiation from radon more than from any other radioactive element. Radon is a colorless, odorless gas that is produced by the radioactive decay of uranium. It is found in small amounts in the soil and can leak into homes and concentrate there, where people breathe it. Radon is the second-leading cause of lung cancer, behind smoking tobacco. The universal use of X-rays in the United States—mostly for necessary diagnostic procedures—means that virtually everyone is exposed to them. Although modern X-ray machines deliver low doses of X-rays, they still present a small risk of causing cancer.

Not all cancers are caused by carcinogens, viruses, or radiation. About 5 to 10 percent of cancers are inherited, as seen by the presence of certain cancers in generation after generation within a family. Mutations in the *RB* and *p53* tumor suppressor genes can be inherited. Women who inherit mutations in the *BRCA1* or *BRCA2* tumor suppressor genes (*BRCA* stands for "breast cancer") have a very high chance—estimated at 30 to 80 percent—of developing breast cancer.

REDUCING CANCER RISK

Many factors that cause cancer are certainly beyond our control. But making certain lifestyle choices and avoiding exposure to cancer-causing agents can significantly reduce the risk of developing cancer (see box on page 26). Tobacco use accounts for about one-third of all cancer deaths, and factors related to nutrition, exercise, and being overweight account for another one-third. Avoiding unhealthy habits and developing healthy ones is effective in reducing the risk of cancer.

◆ HOW TO REDUCE YOUR CANCER RISK

Here are some suggestions for reducing cancer risk from *Cancer and the Environment*, published by the National Cancer Institute:

◆ Don't use tobacco, particularly cigarettes, and avoid secondhand smoke. This is by far the most effective way to prevent cancer.

◆ Lose weight if you are overweight. Avoid fatty foods and exercise regularly.

◆ Eat a variety of vegetables, fruits, and whole grains.

◆ Drink alcohol in moderation.

◆ Avoid excessive sun exposure and avoid tanning beds. Wear clothing that covers as much of the body as possible and use sunscreen.

◆ Avoid viral infections. In addition to AIDS, unsafe sex and drug use by injection can result in infections such as hepatitis B, hepatitis C, and human papillomavirus that can cause cancer.

◆ Check your home for high levels of radon. Installing a special ventilation system can reduce radon levels.

◆ Avoid breathing or having skin contact with household or workplace chemicals, pesticides, and dusts.

SUMMARY

Cancer begins when a single abnormal cell divides and copies itself multiple times. The human body produces 50 billion new cells each day and 50 billion cells die off each day, a normal process. Cancer cells do not die off like other cells, however, and are thus immortal and dubbed "super cells." Also, while normal cells have specific shapes and sizes according to their function in the body, cancer cells have no useful function and no specific shape or size—they are disorganized, jumbled together, and look nothing like normal cells.

2

Diagnosing Cancer

KEY POINTS

- Certain symptoms may be a sign of cancer, but they are more often caused by other, less serious physical ailments. Some symptoms, on the other hand, may not show up for months or even years after the cancer first started growing.

- Based on the patient's age and family history, doctors will first screen for cancer through physical examinations and blood tests (as well as Pap smears, mammograms, prostate exams, and other screens); if something appears suspicious, they will next run specific diagnostic tests such as ultrasounds and MRIs (magnetic resonance imaging).

- The earlier a cancer is diagnosed, the better the chances a person has of successful treatment and a longer rate of survival. Regular visits to a physician are key to maintaining good health.

Janet has begun coughing every day. She is concerned because she doesn't have a cold and the coughing has been going on for over a month. At times she has a pain deep in her chest when she coughs, and she finds herself getting tired easily. Janet smoked cigarettes for about 15 years when she was younger. She never worried about lung cancer, but now, in her late 40s, and with these symptoms, the thought keeps coming into her mind. At her husband's urging, she finally makes an appointment with her doctor. The doctor listens to her breathing with a stethoscope and notices an unusual noise in one lung. He feels the lymph nodes in her neck and finds that they are enlarged. These symptoms are enough for him to decide to order some diagnostic tests.

Does Janet have lung cancer? Her symptoms are suspicious, but they may have other causes. The diagnostic tests will determine whether her fears are justified.

SYMPTOMS OF CANCER

Cancer can grow unnoticed for months or years, but eventually symptoms do appear. When the tumor grows large enough, it can press against and invade other tissues, causing pain, bleeding, and fever. Because these symptoms may not seem severe at first, a person may wait for months before consulting a doctor, hoping that the symptoms will go away. Such a delay allows the cancer to grow and makes it more difficult to treat.

The American Cancer Society has a list of symptoms that may indicate cancer. A person should consult a doctor if any of them appear. Fortunately, most of these symptoms have other causes that are less serious than cancer. Here are some of the symptoms:

- A thickening or lump in the breast or other part of the body

- Recent changes in a wart or mole, or other skin changes

- Changes in bowel or bladder habits

- Indigestion or difficulty in swallowing

- Unusual bleeding or discharge.

EARLY DETECTION OF CANCER

In many cases, cancer can be detected before symptoms appear. Routine screening—looking for signs of cancer in apparently healthy people—can detect cancer early, which means that the treatment will probably be more effective than if the cancer is detected later after symptoms appear (see box on page 32). For example, an X-ray procedure called a **mammogram** can detect abnormalities in the breast that may or may not be cancerous. In a mammogram, the breast is first flattened between two plates (which may be uncomfortable), then X-rays are taken from the top and the side. An abnormality in the breast may simply be a **cyst** or a benign tumor, or it could be cancer. If an abnormality appears, the doctor will order further testing to find out what it is. Women in their 40s and older should have a mammogram every year or two. Most breast cancers are now detected at an early stage, and the **five-year survival rate** for these early cancers is 97 percent.

In 1928, George Papanicolaou of Cornell University discovered that cancer of the cervix (the bottom part of the uterus) in women could be diagnosed by collecting cells from the cervix with a swab and examining them for abnormalities. In the 1940s the Pap smear (named after Papanicolaou) was introduced into medical practice, and it has become a routine cancer screen that is usually done every year in healthy women. Doctors also routinely screen for cancer of the colon and rectum. In a digital rectal exam, the doctor lubricates a finger of the latex glove he or she is wearing and inserts it into the rectum to feel for suspicious areas. This process examines only part of the rectum. For people over the age of 50, a more thorough examination uses a **colonoscope** to directly examine the entire rectum and colon. Noncancerous lumps called **polyps** may be found and removed during this procedure to prevent them from developing into cancer (Figure 2.1).

Aside from screening procedures, a routine physical examination by a doctor may detect the possibility of cancer. The doctor checks visually and with the hand for signs of cancer in the mouth and throat, **thyroid gland**, lymph nodes, skin, female pelvis, male prostate and testicles, and rectum. Blood tests that are routinely ordered with a physical examination include blood counts, **metabolic tests**, and tests for liver, kidney, and thyroid function. A low red blood cell count

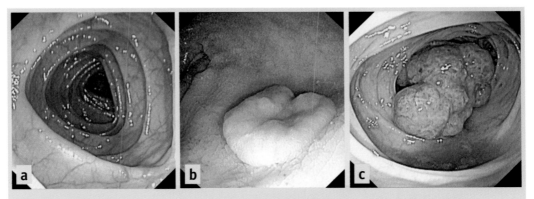

Figure 2.1 (A) A view of a normal colon through a colonoscope. (B) A magnified view of a small, non-cancerous polyp in the colon. Polyps are usually removed to prevent them from developing into cancer. (C) A colon cancer in a 64-year-old man. *(David M. Martin, M.D./Photo Researchers, Inc.)*

◆ IS SCREENING FOR CANCER ALWAYS HELPFUL?

It seems obvious that screening for cancer in apparently healthy people should lower the death toll by detecting cancer early enough to be treated successfully. But screening does present some problems:

◆ Some screening procedures carry a small risk of injury. For example, a routine examination for colon cancer could accidentally perforate (make a hole through) the colon. The patient has only a small chance of having colon cancer, and thus may have suffered an injury without receiving any benefit.

◆ A screening test may produce a false-positive result. This means that cancer is detected, but the test result is wrong and no cancer is actually present. The patient will be very worried and will have to undergo unnecessary testing before the error is discovered.

◆ A screening test may produce a false-negative result: Cancer is not detected, but the patient *does* have cancer. The patient will not be diagnosed and treated for cancer at this point, which reduces the chance for a good outcome when treatment does begin.

◆ Not all cancers turn out to be deadly. A screening test may detect a cancer that might remain small and harmless throughout the person's life. The person will then be burdened with the knowledge that he or she has cancer and may undergo treatment that can have permanent side effects.

Although screening is not perfect, in a large majority of cases a screening test is accurate and produces an accurate result. The benefits of a screening test far outweigh the possible problems associated with it.

indicates **anemia**. Elevated levels of **bilirubin** can mean liver disease and elevated levels of **creatinine** can mean kidney disease. These abnormal test results can have many causes, and are not specific indicators of cancer.

DIAGNOSTIC TESTS

If the doctor finds anything suspicious during the physical examination, the routine blood test results, or a screening procedure, he or she orders one or more specific diagnostic tests and procedures that are performed by specialists: imaging techniques, detection of chemicals called **tumor markers**, **biopsy**, **endoscopy**, and **cytology**.

Imaging techniques that can show a tumor include the familiar X-rays used for a mammogram and newer methods such as **computerized tomography** (CT) scans, **magnetic resonance imaging** (MRI), **ultrasound**, and the use of radioactive **isotopes**. Tumors are usually denser than the surrounding tissue and absorb more X-rays, and thus appear as a lighter area on X-ray film. Newer X-ray techniques can detect cancers better than standard X-rays. For example, a CT scan uses a computer-controlled X-ray machine that directs very thin X-ray beams at different angles to make a three-dimensional image of the chest or abdomen or any part of the body being studied (Figure 2.2).

An MRI image is produced by a machine that uses strong magnetic fields and radio waves to excite the nucleus of the hydrogen atoms in body tissue to a higher energy level. The hydrogen atoms give off their energy when the radio waves are turned off, and this energy is recorded and used to construct an image (Figure 2.3). Tumors contain more water (H_2O) than normal tissue, and thus give off a stronger signal. MRI is particularly useful for detecting cancers of the brain and spinal cord.

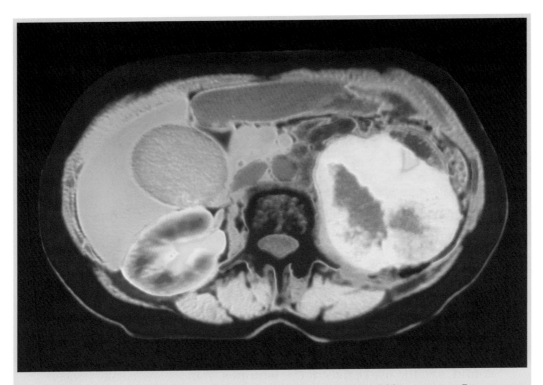

Figure 2.2 A computerized tomography (CT) scan showing kidney cancer. Every person has two kidneys. The kidney on the lower left (colored red) is a normal kidney. The enlarged kidney on the right (yellow and blue) is cancerous, and cannot function normally. Other organs that can be seen in this CT scan are the liver (green, on the left) and gall bladder (blue, on the left). A vertebra (rust colored), which is part of the backbone, is in the center. *(SPL/Photo Researchers, Inc.)*

Ultrasound imaging sends sound waves through the skin into the body. The sound waves bounce off different tissues in different ways and are recorded as an image that can be examined for suspicious areas.

Radioactive isotopes can be used to form an image of a cancer. A radioactive isotope is linked to a chemical compound. The radioactive compound is then given to the patient by mouth or **intravenously**, into a vein. As the radioactive compound circulates through the body, it accumulates in the cancer differently from how it accumulates in normal organ tissue. For example, liver cancer cells do not take up the compound used for imaging liver cancer, whereas normal liver cells do. In contrast, bone cancer cells absorb the compound used for imaging bone cancer, and the cancer shows up as a "hot spot." A machine makes an image of the radiation given off by the isotope, and cancer shows up as different from the surrounding tissue.

Developed in the 1970s, **positron emission tomography (PET)** is a more recent process that uses radioactive isotopes. A common PET scan procedure uses a sugar called fluorodeoxyglucose (*fluoro* = a fluorine atom; *deoxyglucose* = a sugar molecule) that contains the radioactive isotope fluorine-18. This sugar is used to diagnose lung cancer. The sugar is injected intravenously and is absorbed rapidly by cancer cells because they have a fast **metabolism**. The radiation from the cancer cells is recorded by repeated scanning, and a computer uses all the scans to construct a three-dimensional image that shows the location of the cancer.

Tumor markers are chemicals, typically proteins, produced by cancer tumors that can be detected in blood and tissue. If a physical examination and routine blood tests arouse suspicion, the doctor may order one or more tumor marker tests. There is no single tumor marker test that can be used for all types of cancer—each test is specific to a certain kind of cancer. A tumor marker called carcinoembryonic antigen is elevated in people with colorectal, lung, breast, and pancreas cancers. Prostate-specific antigen is elevated in men with prostate cancer. Cancer antigen 125 is elevated in women with cancer of the **ovary**. As with routine blood tests, however, other conditions besides cancer can cause elevated levels of tumor markers.

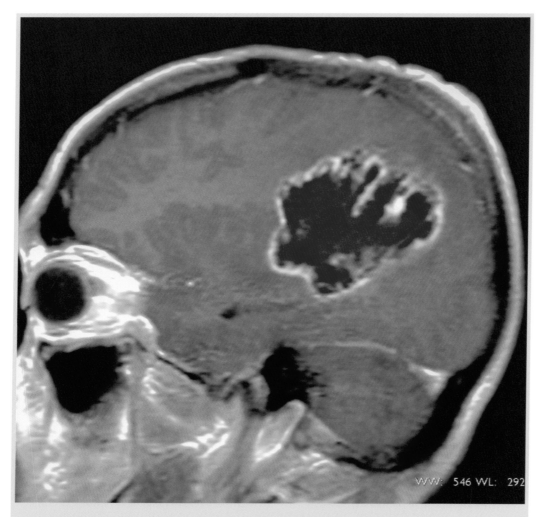

Figure 2.3 A magnetic resonance imaging (MRI) scan of the head showing brain cancer. (*BSIP/Photo Researchers,Inc.*)

In addition to imaging techniques and tumor marker tests, a doctor can look directly for cancer in certain organs by using various kinds of endoscopes. An endoscope is a narrow, flexible fiber-optic tube that transmits an image through the tube and then through a lens to the doctor, similar to a microscope. Some endoscopes have a small camera that lets the doctor see the images on a large screen. An endoscope is inserted into an opening in the body like the mouth or through an incision. It can examine a suspicious area detected by other tests or determine the exact location of a tumor before surgery. The doctor can see a suspected tumor and remove a sample for testing. Different endo-scopes include the **cystoscope**, which is inserted through the urethra to observe the urinary tract and bladder; the colonoscope, which is inserted through the rectum to examine the colon (Figure 2.4, B); and the **bronchoscope**, which is inserted through the mouth or nose to examine the lungs (Figure 2.4, A).

Another diagnostic test is cytology, in which a doctor collects cells and another doctor, called a **pathologist**, examines them for signs of cancer. Cell samples can be obtained in several ways. The doctor can scrape cells from tissue, either directly or with an endoscope. For example, a doctor doing a Pap smear uses a spatula or brush to remove cells directly from the cervix. The doctor can also get cells from body fluids, such as urine or fluids around the lungs. Fine needle aspiration uses a very thin needle to withdraw cells from a suspected tumor. The cells are put on slides, stained to make the internal structures of the cells more visible, and examined by the pathologist under a microscope to determine whether they are cancerous.

In a process called a biopsy, a doctor removes a relatively large sample of a suspected tumor for examination under the microscope. Imaging techniques, tumor markers, or cytology may strongly suggest cancer, but they may not be conclusive. Biopsy is the most accurate way to determine whether someone has cancer. The doctor removes the

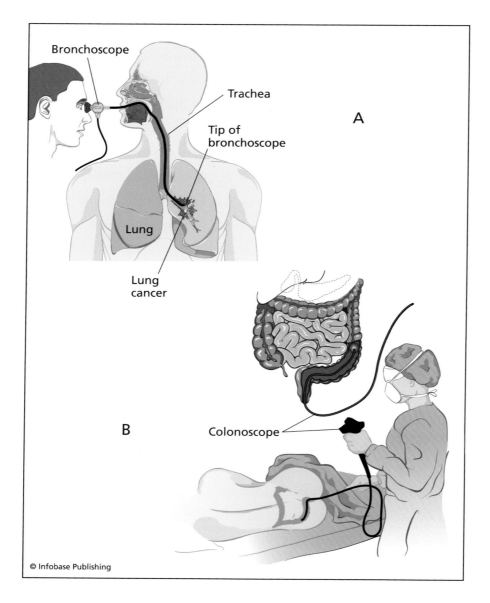

Figure 2.4 (A) A doctor using a bronchoscope to examine a patient's lungs for cancer. (B) A doctor using a colonoscope to examine a patient's colon for cancer.

tissue sample with a large needle or an endoscope, or by cutting out a piece of the tumor or the entire tumor through surgery.

Surgical biopsies are more serious procedures than needle biopsies and endoscope biopsies, and may require general **anesthesia** for the patient. For example, a **laparotomy** involves making an incision to open up the abdomen to expose a suspicious mass. If cancer is found, a separate operation later removes it or another therapy is used. At times a part of the tumor is removed and sent for analysis while the patient remains on the operating table. The pathologist quickly examines the tissue, taking 10 to 20 minutes. If the diagnosis is cancer, the tumor is immediately removed. At other times, the doctor simply removes the entire tumor during the biopsy if it is small and easy to reach, such as cancers of the skin or mouth, even though the tumor has not yet been confirmed as cancer.

THE PATHOLOGIST'S DIAGNOSIS

The pathologist first examines the biopsy sample without using a microscope, noting the sample's size and shape (if it is the entire tumor), color, and whether it has a well-defined border. Frequently the overall appearance gives a clue as to whether the sample is cancerous. The biopsy sample is then placed in hot wax. When it cools, the solid block is cut into thin slices with an instrument called a microtome; then it is stained and examined under a microscope.

The pathologist looks for characteristics of cancer when examining the cells under the microscope. Cancer cells may be larger or smaller than normal cells, or may have a different shape. The nucleus of a cancer cell is abnormal—typically it is larger than normal because it contains more DNA than a normal cell does. Cells in normal tissue have a useful function, and they are found in regular arrangements that help them perform their function. By contrast, cancer cells do not have a useful function and are found in irregular clumps.

If the entire tumor has been removed, the pathologist examines the borders of the sample to determine whether any cancer cells were left behind in the body. If cancer cells at the edge of the tumor have layers of normal cells on the outside, then the cancer has probably not spread into the surrounding tissue.

If the pathologist decides that the cells are cancerous, he or she then describes the cancer in detail. Cancer is classified by where it is located in the body and how it appears to the pathologist examining it through a microscope. The first classification is according to the type of tissue the cancer develops in. **Carcinomas** are the most common cancers, accounting for 80 to 90 percent of cancers. They occur in the **epithelium**—the skin and the thin layer of tissue that lines the inside and outside of organs found in the gastrointestinal track (gut), the respiratory track, and the reproductive organs. Carcinomas are found in the skin, breast, lung, colon, rectum, cervix, stomach, and many other organs. **Sarcomas** are cancers of the connective or supportive tissue in bones, tendons, muscle, and fat. **Leukemias** are cancers of the **bone marrow**, the cells that produce blood cells. (Bone marrow is the soft, sponge-like tissue in the center of bones.) **Myelomas** are cancers of the bone marrow cells that produce **antibodies**, the proteins of the immune system that attack bacteria, viruses, and other foreign invaders (see Chapter 7). **Lymphomas** are cancers of the lymph nodes.

The pathologist also notes the body site where the cancer first appeared, such as the breast, prostate, lung, or colon. No matter where the cancer has spread, the cancer is described in terms of its primary site. For example, a prostate cancer that has spread to the spine is still called prostate cancer. The cancer cells will behave like prostate cancer cells, not bone cancer cells.

The pathologist gives the cancer a grade (1 to 3) that describes how closely it resembles normal cells. Cancer cells that resemble normal cells are low grade. Those that do not resemble normal cells are high grade. High-grade cancer cells tend to grow and spread more rapidly than low-grade cells.

Perhaps most important of all, the pathologist determines the stage of the cancer (see box on page 42). The stage is usually labeled by one of five numbers, 0 to IV, and describes how dangerous the cancer is by noting the size of tumor and whether it has spread from the original site. The characteristics of each stage vary with the type of cancer, but in general, a stage 0 cancer is *in situ,* which means that it has not grown beyond the layer of cells where it began. A stage I cancer is larger, perhaps 0.75 inch (2 or more cm) across, but has not spread outside the organ where it was first located. Stages II and III cancers have spread to nearby sites. A stage IV cancer has metastasized to distant parts of the body.

The pathologist's overall description of the cancer, particularly the cancer's stage, largely determines what the course of treatment will be. In prostate cancer, for example, a stage I cancer can be treated surgically by removing the prostate, but a stage III cancer will be treated with radiation or hormone therapy. The accuracy of the pathologist's diagnosis is the key to successful treatment of a patient's cancer.

SUMMARY

Regular visits to the doctor and routine screenings can help detect cancer early. During physical exams, doctors will check patients (visually and by hand) for cancer in the mouth and throat, thyroid gland, lymph

♦ STAGING CANCER

The TNM staging system is used for many cancers that form a solid tumor. It is based on the following characteristics:

♦ The size of the *tumor* (T = 0 to 4, with 4 being the largest)

♦ The degree of spread, if any, to the lymph *nodes* (N = 0 to 3)

♦ Whether the cancer has *metastasized* to other organs (M = 0 or 1)

For example, a T2, N1, M0 breast cancer tumor could mean a 0.75- to 2-inch (2- to 5-cm) tumor that has spread to nearby lymph nodes in the armpit but has not metastasized to other organs. The overall TNM stage of a tumor is summarized as a stage 0, I, II, III, or IV cancer, with stage IV being the most serious. A T1, N0, M0 tumor is stage I; a T2, N1, M0 tumor is stage III; and any M1 tumor is stage IV.

The TNM system is not used for all cancers. Leukemias, for example, usually do not form solid tumors and require a different classification system.

node, skin, and more. They will also run blood tests for blood counts and to ensure that certain organs are functioning properly. If the doctor sees something suspicious during the exam and from the blood test results, the next step may be a diagnostic test, such as an ultrasound, MRI, or biopsy. Doctors can also use endoscopes (long, flexible tubes that transmit images) to look directly at organs for cancer. Pathologists examine cells taken during a biopsy for cancer; if cancer is found, they give it a "grade" number based on how closely it resembles normal cells and a "stage" number based on its size and if it has spread.

3

DECIDING ON TREATMENT

KEY POINTS

- Treatment for cancer varies for each person due to a variety of factors, ranging from the type of cancer, its size, and how advanced it is, to the person's overall health and his or her ability to tolerate certain side effects.

- Surgery, radiation therapy, and chemotherapy are the most frequent treatments for cancer, with surgery being the most successful if the cancer is isolated in a small area. A combination of the three is often used in treating cancer.

- Doctors will recommend treatment options to patients and provide literature and resources to help educate patients about their specific type of cancer. Patients who want to be fully informed and comfortable in their decisions can take further steps by getting opinions from other doctors, researching their disease by reading books and looking up information on medical Web sites, and discussing their options with family members and friends.

Treating cancer has a simple goal: to get rid of the cancer tumor and prevent it from returning. But deciding how to treat a patient's cancer is often difficult and complex. Why? The same type of cancer is different from patient to patient because people are not all the same. They have different genes and slightly different molecular and cellular processes. Also, cells from the same type of cancer found in different patients are not identical. These differences between patients and between cancer cells means that treatment is not an exact science, and the results of treatment may be unpredictable.

Doctors take many factors into account when recommending a treatment. The type of cancer and its stage—its size and whether it has spread—are the most important factors. A small tumor may simply be removed, but a tumor that has metastasized will require other, more aggressive treatment. The doctor must consider the age and health of the patient and his or her ability to tolerate an aggressive treatment that has serious side effects. Once the characteristics of the cancer and of the patient are known, then several treatments or combinations of treatments can be considered.

CANCER TREATMENTS

The most frequent cancer treatments are surgery, radiation therapy, and chemotherapy. Surgery—cutting out the cancer—is the most successful treatment if the tumor has not spread and can be removed without damaging organs or causing other problems. A surgeon will remove the tumor and some of the tissue surrounding it, and perhaps remove nearby lymph nodes because the cancer may have spread there.

Radiation therapy—bombarding cancer with X-rays, subatomic particle beams, or particles from radioactive isotopes—shrinks tumors by damaging the cancer cells' DNA, thus disrupting their reproduction. Like surgery, it is used to treat cancer that has not spread or has spread only to nearby tissues. The radiation will damage both cancer cells and normal tissue cells. Depending on the part of the body treated, radiation therapy can cause burning of the skin, nausea, vomiting, diarrhea, and loss of hair.

Chemotherapy uses drugs to treat cancer that has spread to different parts of the body through the blood or the **lymphatic system**—the system of lymph nodes, organs, and thin tubes that produce lymph fluid (a colorless fluid containing white blood cells) and transports it throughout the body. Different chemotherapy drugs work in different ways to kill cancer cells. They can damage cancer cells' DNA, prevent cell division, and disrupt cell growth. Like radiation therapy, chemotherapy kills normal cells as well as cancer cells, and the side effects are similar to those of radiation therapy. Surgery, radiation therapy, and chemotherapy are frequently used in combination.

A different type of **oncologist** (a doctor who treats cancer) performs each type of treatment. A surgical oncologist performs surgery to remove the primary tumor (the original tumor), but the surgery may leave behind cancer cells in nearby tissues. A radiation oncologist then uses radiation therapy to kill these cancer cells. A medical oncologist uses chemotherapy to kill cancer cells that may have spread from the primary tumor to other parts of the body. For example, cancer of the ovary is usually treated by surgery to remove one or both ovaries, plus the **uterus** and nearby lymph nodes if the cancer has spread there. Chemotherapy is usually started a few weeks after surgery to kill cancer cells that may have spread from the ovaries to the abdomen, liver, and intestines. Less frequently, radiation therapy is used to kill cancer cells that have spread from the ovaries to nearby tissues in the abdomen.

In addition to oncologists, other health-care professionals are part of a cancer treatment team. A nurse who specializes in cancer can administer chemotherapy and treat side effects. Cancer and its treatment can cause weight loss, nausea, and loss of appetite, so a dietician designs a diet that will help the patient recover. A physical therapist works with the patient to restore functions like walking, normal muscular strength, and flexibility that may have been lost as a result of cancer that damages tissue or the cancer treatment itself. If needed, a psychologist or other type of counselor helps the patient and his or her family deal with emotional problems.

MAKING THE TREATMENT DECISION

Because cancer is a complex disease, no two cancers or cancer patients are alike. Consequently treatment plans must be tailored to the individual patient. Cancer may or may not follow a predictable path of growth and may or may not respond to a treatment as expected. In many cases there is no obvious best choice. Because of these factors the cancer patient is more involved in making treatment decisions than with many other diseases.

Many people think of cancer as a death sentence. Upon hearing the diagnosis of cancer, people may experience many emotions: fear, panic, numbness, disbelief. In addition to thinking about dying at some point in the near future, they may worry about the immediate effect of the illness on their families and on their ability to work. In order to think clearly, patients need to overcome the fear of cancer and of the side effects of treatment. They must be sure to understand what the doctor is explaining: how advanced the cancer is, what the treatment options are, and what the side effects of each treatment are. Cancer patients can bring along a family member or friend to a meeting with the doctor and take notes. The doctor may give the patient pamphlets or handouts about the type of cancer in question. Numerous books on cancer are available from public libraries and bookstores. Patients can also get up-to-date information on the Internet from the American Cancer Society or the National Cancer Institute.

Many patients are not confident about discussing their condition with doctors. The patients think they cannot understand detailed medical information, and so they simply let the doctor present treatment options for them to consider. Other patients will gather detailed information on their own about their cancer and possible treatments, and perhaps consult several doctors. In either case, patients and their families should weigh the advantages and disadvantages of each type of treatment and make decisions with the help of a doctor.

All patients hope that treatment will cure their cancer. But patients need to understand what is realistic to expect from a treatment. Even though the cancer has been treated, the outcome is not predictable. The cancer may seem to disappear, only to return some years later. Perhaps the best attitude for a patient to have is that cancer is a chronic disease—a long-term disease—that can be managed like other diseases such as **diabetes** and heart disease, even if it can't be cured. Cancer patients can lead long, active lives.

Is it realistic for a patient to hope for a cure? For some cancers, such as a small skin melanoma that has not metastasized, the answer is yes. The melanoma can be removed by surgery and it will probably not return. But for other cancers, such as a melanoma that has metastasized, the goal of treatment is to cause the cancer to go into **remission**, where the cancer seems to disappear or at least shrink in size. A remission may last for only a few months or for many years, after which the cancer begins to grow again. Although it is not a cure, remission can give the patient additional years of life.

The patient should consider the risks and side effects of each treatment option compared to its benefit. For example, chemotherapy may promise a chance at a complete cure, but the toxic drugs it uses can cause great pain and might actually kill the patient. Surgery for some cancers can seriously affect how people think about themselves and their lives. For example, a total **mastectomy** for advanced breast cancer involves the complete removal of the breast. This can have a devastating psychological impact on the affected woman.

Treatment choices are even more difficult in the case of an advanced cancer that has metastasized to many parts of the body with little or no hope for a cure. Is it worth suffering the severe side effects of an aggressive chemotherapy treatment to extend life? Or would the patient be better off with less time to live, but less suffering during that time?

Generally, the more aggressive treatments have a higher success rate, but the patient may not be willing to pay the higher price of severe or permanent side effects such as disfigurement caused by surgery. Many women with breast cancer choose breast conservation surgery, which removes less breast tissue, instead of total mastectomy. With all cancers, patients will have their own way of thinking about the treatment options and will have to make their own decisions with the help of a their families and their doctors.

Champion bicycle racer Lance Armstrong (see Chapter 1) had a difficult decision to make when he was diagnosed with cancer in 1996. If he had agreed to undergo the standard chemotherapy for his cancer, it would have damaged his lungs and ended his cycling career. Instead, he opted for a different treatment that did not damage his lungs. It worked for him. His cancer has been in remission since the end of 1996.

SUMMARY

Each person is unique, made of cells and genes that are different from other people; thus a cancer treatment for one patient may not work as well for another patient with the same cancer. The type of cancer a person has, coupled with its size and stage of development, as well as the person's age and general health, each contribute to the doctor's recommendations for treatment options. Surgery, radiation therapy, and chemotherapy are usually the options offered, either alone or in combination. Oncologists, doctors who specialize in treating cancer, perform the treatments. Patients can participate fully in deciding on their course of treatment by researching their disease and seeking opinions from other doctors.

4

CUTTING OUT TUMORS: SURGERY

KEY POINTS

♦ Although an ancient form of treatment, today surgery is performed on over 50 percent of all cancer patients. It is used to perform biopsies, remove tumors, and reduce pain.

♦ Thanks to innovators in the mid-19th century, anesthesia has helped patients feel no pain during surgical procedures, and antiseptic practices in hospitals have greatly reduced the risk of infection during operations.

♦ During surgery, doctors can examine the diseased tissue once it is removed to determine if the cancer is contained or if it has spread and if further treatment is needed.

Surgery—cutting out tumors—is the oldest treatment for cancer. It was described by the Roman doctor Celsus 2,000 years ago. Surgery of any kind was horrifyingly painful until 1846, when a dramatic demonstration by Boston dentist William Morton during surgery to remove a tumor from the face of a patient showed that breathing an **anesthetic** called ether could put patients to sleep for the entire operation (see box on page 52). William Halsted pioneered one of the first successful surgeries for cancer—the mastectomy for breast cancer—in the 1890s. His technique removed the breast, the muscles in the chest, and the lymph nodes under the arm. It was used until the 1970s, when doctors found that less drastic surgery was also successful.

Despite being an ancient treatment, over half of today's cancer patients will undergo surgery. Surgery has several uses in treating cancer. It can prevent a cancer from developing by removing **lesions**, such as polyps in the colon and suspicious skin moles, before they have a chance to turn into cancer. During a biopsy to diagnose a possible cancer, a surgeon removes a sample of the tumor tissue to examine. Once cancer is diagnosed, a surgeon can remove the tumor, the surrounding tissue, and perhaps nearby lymph nodes, which can rid the patient of cancer if it has not metastasized. A pathologist later examines the surrounding tissue, called the **margin**, to see whether it is free of cancer. If not, radiation therapy or chemotherapy may be started.

After surgery to remove a tumor, more surgery may be needed to make the patient more comfortable about his or her appearance, like reconstructing a missing breast, or restoring a function such as the ability to swallow food. If the cancer cannot be cured, surgery for **palliation**—relieving pain or other discomfort—may be performed, even though the patient will eventually die of the cancer. For example, a tumor can block the intestine and prevent food from passing through. Palliative surgery may remove enough of the tumor to restore digestion.

◆ THE TANGLED HISTORY OF ANESTHESIA

Until the middle of the 19th century, patients agreed to have surgery only if they were desperate and brave. Many patients chose to die rather than go through the agonizing pain of surgery. At the time, there was no way to prevent pain, and patients had to endure procedures such as amputation of a leg while fully conscious and tied down. A surgeon was considered good only if he worked quickly. Beginning in the 1840s, a tangled series of events led to the use of chemicals called anesthetics to control pain.

Crawford Long, a Georgia doctor, used a chemical called ether in 1842 to put a patient to sleep while he removed a tumor from the patient's neck. The patient breathed ether that was dripped onto a cloth covering his face. Long did not publicize his accomplishment. Other men who tried to solve the problem of pain were not so modest.

In 1844 Connecticut dentist Horace Wells performed an experiment on himself. He had another dentist give him the gas nitrous oxide to breathe while a troublesome tooth was pulled. Wells felt no pain, and began to use nitrous oxide on his own patients. In 1845, Wells demonstrated his discovery at Massachusetts General Hospital. But the patient groaned when Wells pulled his tooth, and the audience jeered at Wells.

Boston dentist William Morton had better luck. Morton was Wells's former partner and had seen the failed demonstration. In 1846 he set up another demonstration at the same hospital in which he had a patient breathe ether while a surgeon removed a tumor from his neck. The operation was a success, and the news spread quickly. Morton refused to tell anyone what chemical he had used to put the patient to sleep. He called it "Letheon," and tried unsuccessfully to make money from it. But the anesthesia was quickly discovered to be ether, and doctors everywhere soon began using it.

But Morton had a problem. Charles Jackson, a doctor, had suggested using ether to Morton, and now he wanted credit for this discovery. Morton

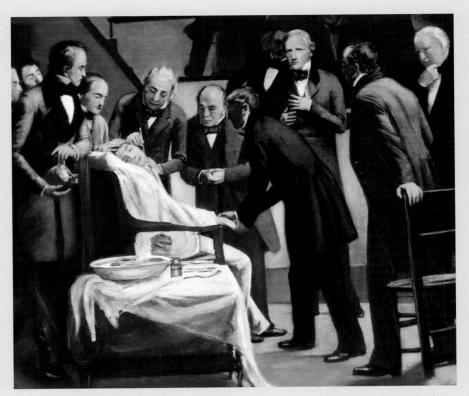

Figure 4.1 Part of the painting "First Operation with Ether" by Robert Hinckley. The patient has been put to sleep with ether, and a tumor is being removed from his neck. This momentous event in medicine occurred at Massachusetts General Hospital in 1846. (*Bettman/Corbis*)

(continues)

(continued)

and Jackson fought for years in and out of court. Meanwhile, Wells also tried to take credit for the use of ether.

None of the three men fared well. After his failed demonstration in 1845, Wells began experimenting on himself with various chemicals and became addicted to chloroform, another anesthetic. He was imprisoned for throwing acid in the face of a prostitute, and committed suicide in jail in 1848. Morton spent all his money fighting Jackson and died poor in 1868. Jackson went insane and spent his last years in an asylum before dying in 1880. Unlike the other three men, Crawford Long did not try to make money from his discovery, and seems to have led a satisfying life.

The use of anesthesia became fully accepted when the English doctor John Snow gave chloroform to Queen Victoria during the birth of her eighth child in 1853. Since then, anesthesia has developed into a medical specialty with many anesthetics, different techniques to administer them, and sophisticated technology to monitor patients during the millions of surgeries that are performed each year.

TYPES OF SURGERY

Surgeons still cut out cancers the old-fashioned way using a scalpel—a sharp knife—but newer methods are now available to treat certain cancers. **Cryosurgery** (*cryo* means "cold") kills cancer cells with extreme cold (Figure 4.2). The surgeon first inserts a hollow steel tube called a cryoprobe into the tumor, using ultrasound to guide the placement. The surgeon then pumps liquid nitrogen (-196°C [-321°F]) through the probe to freeze and destroy the tumor, and uses ultrasound to monitor

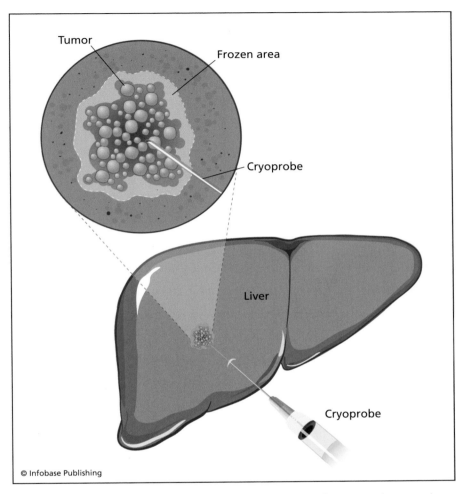

Figure 4.2 Using cryosurgery to destroy a liver tumor. The cyroprobe contains liquid nitrogen (-196°C) that freezes the tumor without damaging too much of the normal liver tissue.

the freezing to avoid damaging too much of the normal tissue around the tumor. After the cryosurgery, the frozen tumor gradually thaws, then slowly breaks down and is absorbed by the body. Compared to normal surgery, cryosurgery causes less bleeding and pain because it only requires a small incision through the skin and muscles, rather than a larger incision to make room for the surgeon's hands and instruments to enter the body. Cryosurgery, however, is not a replacement for traditional surgery. It can only be used for certain kinds of tumors, such as those of the liver and prostate, and experts are not yet certain whether it is as effective as traditional surgery.

Another newer surgical technique uses lasers to destroy tumors. Laser light is a narrow beam of light of a single wavelength, rather than the many wavelengths found in natural light. Laser light can concentrate high energy in a tiny spot. A flexible endoscope is used to transmit the laser light through fiber optics to the tumor. Like cryosurgery, laser therapy is used for only a few kinds of cancers, such as skin cancers and some small cancers inside the body. It can also be used as a palliative treatment—for example, to destroy a tumor that is blocking the **esophagus**.

Surgery is frequently combined with other treatments, such as radiation therapy and chemotherapy, because one type of treatment alone may not be effective. Surgery can remove the main tumor, radiation can destroy cancer cells left behind in nearby tissues, and chemotherapy can kill cancer cells that have spread through the blood and lymphatic system.

SIDE EFFECTS OF SURGERY

Surgery for cancer can leave permanent changes in how the body looks and functions. A surgery for colon cancer called a **colostomy** removes part of the colon and creates an opening, called a **stoma**, in the abdomen. Waste that was once excreted through the anus now leaves the body through the stoma and is collected in a bag. A radical **prostatectomy**—the removal of a male patient's prostate gland—can eliminate a prostate cancer that has not spread. But the surgery can cause the patient to permanently lose control of his bladder and have to wear pads at all times to absorb leaking urine; also, this patient may no longer be able to have sexual intercourse because he can no longer have an erection. Dealing with the emotional impact caused by surgery can be as important as dealing with the physical changes (see Chapter 9).

LISA'S SURGERY

"I'm afraid you have cancer," Dr. Stewart told Lisa. Fifty-three-year-old Lisa had been having slight bleeding from the vagina off and on for several months before she made an appointment with Dr. Stewart, her **gynecologist**. After considering possible causes, Dr. Stewart decided to do a biopsy of the **endometrium**—the lining of the uterus—to check for cancer. She scraped some tissue from the endometrium and sent it to the laboratory for diagnosis. The uterus (also called the womb) is a hollow organ shaped like a pear where the developing fetus grows until it is ready to be born (Figure 4.4). A fallopian tube and an ovary are attached to each side of the uterus. An ovary produces an egg, which moves through the fallopian tube. The egg is fertilized in the fallopian tube and then implants itself in the uterus and develops into a fetus. The bottom of the uterus, the cervix, is attached to the vagina, through which the baby will be delivered. Because Lisa was over 50 years old and had gone through menopause (the natural stopping of menstruation), her chances of developing endometrial cancer were much greater than when she was younger. The results from the pathologist confirmed Dr. Stewart's suspicion: Lisa had endometrial cancer. The pathologist determined that the cancer cells were grade 1, meaning that they more closely resembled normal cells than advanced cancer cells. This was good news.

◆ KILLING THE KILLERS

Half of all surgery patients in the middle of the 19th century died after surgery. They did not die from the surgery itself, but from what was called "hospital disease." The surgical wound would become inflamed and an expanding area of tissue would die, eventually leading to an agonizing death. Hospitals gained a reputation as a place to die, rather than be cured.

England's Joseph Lister changed that. In the 1860s Louis Pasteur of France showed that small **organisms** caused decay. Lister learned of Pasteur's work and realized that "hospital disease" was likely caused by similar organisms. He needed a way to kill them before they killed the patient. Lister had already heard of a chemical called carbolic acid being used to treat sewage, and began experimenting with it in surgery. In August 1865 he first used carbolic acid in surgery on the wound of a boy with a severe leg fracture. The leg healed and the boy survived.

Lister experimented by putting carbolic acid directly on surgical wounds and spraying it into the air in the operating room to kill the organisms. Although the carbolic acid killed the organisms, which we now know are bacteria, the harsh chemical burned the wound and the doctor's skin and lungs. Lister then designed a cloth bandage containing carbolic acid mixed with other substances. The bandage kept bacteria out of the wound without burning it. He also treated surgical instruments with carbolic acid and insisted that doctors wash their hands thoroughly. Today, we know that "hospital disease" is actually infection, and we know that the organisms that cause it are different kinds of bacteria.

In 1867 Lister announced to the British Medical Association that he had greatly reduced infection and death from surgery. But he had a difficult time convincing doctors to follow his procedures, and some even ridiculed him. It seemed ridiculous that tiny bacteria, invisible to the naked eye, could kill a person. At the time doctors did not wash their hands thoroughly, and surgical instruments were simply wiped off and used on the

Figure 4.3 Joseph Lister. (*U.S. National Library of Medicine*)

next patient. The floor of the operating room was frequently covered with blood, urine, and pus, and the air stank.

Even though Lister had a hard time convincing doctors in England, his ideas quickly spread to the rest of Europe. Gradually the rest of the world adopted his techniques, and deaths from infections caused by surgery became much less frequent. Today hospitals are careful to use **antiseptic** (*anti* means "against" and *sepsis* means "destruction of tissue") practices everywhere, not just in surgery.

Endometrial cancer accounts for about 6 percent of all cancer in women in the United States—there are nearly 40,000 new cases each year. If not detected and treated early, it can spread to nearby tissues in the vagina, fallopian tubes, and ovaries. Advanced endometrial cancer can spread further to the bladder and bowel. If detected before it has spread, patients with endometrial cancer have a 96 percent five-year survival rate.

Dr. Stewart referred Lisa to Dr. Rodriguez, a surgical oncologist with experience treating endometrial cancer. Dr. Rodriguez explained to Lisa that he would perform a **hysterectomy**—an operation to remove the uterus. In addition, he would remove the fallopian tubes, ovaries, and nearby lymph nodes because it was possible that the cancer had spread to those places. Another reason to remove the ovaries is that they secrete **estrogen**, a **hormone**, which can cause any inactive cancer cells left behind by surgery to begin dividing. After the uterus was removed during the surgery, a pathologist would examine it to determine how deep into the wall of the uterus the cancer had penetrated. If the cancer is confined to the uterus—a stage I cancer—the surgery would end at this point. If the cancer had spread, however, other tissue would also be removed and the surgery would be followed by radiation therapy.

Dr. Rodriguez explained the risks of the surgery to Lisa. As with any serious surgery, Lisa could possibly experience excessive bleeding, damage to organs and blood vessels, a negative reaction to the anesthesia, and problems with the heart, lungs, or kidneys. He reassured her that these problems are rare. He told her the surgery would leave a scar. Before the surgery, Lisa would be given an informed consent form to sign. This form states what surgery is being performed, and its benefits and risks. Signing the form meant that Lisa understood all the risks and gave her permission for the surgery to be performed.

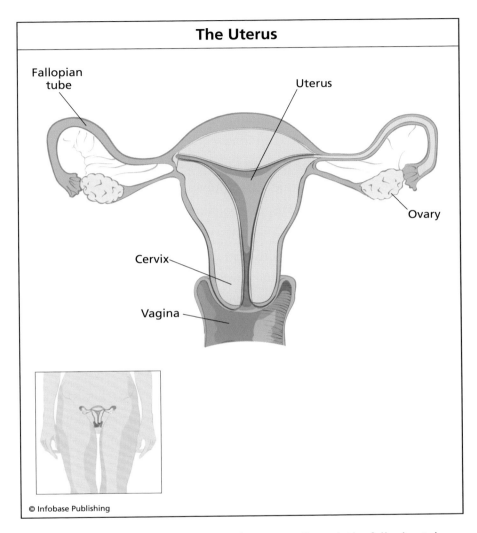

The Uterus

Fallopian tube

Uterus

Ovary

Cervix

Vagina

© Infobase Publishing

Figure 4.4 An ovary produces an egg that moves through the fallopian tube, where it is fertilized. The egg implants itself in the uterus, a hollow organ where the baby grows until it is born by being pushed through the vagina.

Lisa was in good health and did not have any conditions such as diabetes or high blood pressure that might cause problems during the surgery. About a week before the surgery, Lisa had blood and urine tests done to see if she had any risk of excessive bleeding or abnormal liver or kidney function. She also had an X-ray to check her lungs and an **electrocardiogram** to check her heart. Her blood type was determined in case she needed a blood transfusion during the surgery.

On the morning of Lisa's surgery, she was put on a gurney, a bed with wheels. A nurse inserted an intravenous (IV) line—a small plastic tube—into a vein in Lisa's arm so that she could receive medications and fluid during the operation. Lisa's pubic area was shaved to remove hair and cleaned with an antiseptic solution.

At the scheduled time Lisa's gurney was wheeled into the operating room. She was transferred to the operating table and laid on her back. In addition to Dr. Rodriguez, the surgical team in the operating room included an assistant surgeon, an **anesthesiologist**, and three nurses to handle instruments and supplies.

The operation began with the anesthesiologist injecting a drug into the intravenous line in Lisa's arm. Lisa fell asleep within a few seconds. The anesthesiologist then fed an **endotracheal tube** down Lisa's throat to keep the airway to her lungs open. The anesthesiologist would administer an anesthetic gas through the endotracheal tube during the operation to keep Lisa asleep. The anesthetic would enter the bloodstream through the lungs and be carried to the brain. The anesthesiologist would continually monitor Lisa's heart rate, blood pressure, breathing, and blood oxygen level until the operation was over. A nurse inserted a **catheter**—a long, narrow plastic tube—up through the **urethra** and into the bladder so that urine would automatically drain from the bladder.

Dr. Rodriguez made a 6-inch (15 cm) incision through the layers of skin, fat, and muscle from just below Lisa's navel down to the pubic bone. The incision was spread and kept open with a tool called a retractor to create a large working area. Dr. Rodriguez cut the blood vessels and **ligaments** that are attached to the uterus and tied off the blood vessels to prevent bleeding. He then cut below the cervix to separate the uterus from the vagina, and removed the uterus, fallopian tubes, and ovaries. He finished by removing lymph nodes that were near the uterus.

Dr. Rodriguez examined the uterus and other tissues that he had removed and saw that they did not seem to show that cancer had spread outside the uterus. A pathologist in the operating room immediately examined the uterus more closely, cutting it in half and looking at parts of it under a microscope. He found that the cancer was indeed confined to the inner layer of the uterus. This meant that no further surgery was needed. Dr. Rodriguez then sewed the top of the vagina shut, removed the retractors, and sewed the incision shut. The pathologist later examined the lymph nodes that Dr. Rodriguez removed and found no signs of cancer.

Lisa was taken to the recovery room and stayed there for two hours until the anesthesia wore off and she woke up. After she was moved to her own hospital room, she was shown how to operate a pump so she could give herself morphine intravenously to relieve pain. Lisa was able to stand up that night, and she began walking the next day. She went home five days after surgery and was almost completely recovered in six weeks. Because Lisa's endometrial cancer was treated at a very early stage, she has an excellent chance of being completely cured.

SUMMARY

Before the 1850s, doctors took their scalpels to patients who were wide awake and strapped down to reduce thrashing. Surgery was not for the faint of heart in those days. Since then, however, anesthesia is administered, which causes patients to sleep through surgery and feel no pain. Infection is also greatly reduced due to the development of antiseptic practices in hospitals. Surgery is often used as one part of a three-pronged approach to treating cancer, along with radiation therapy and chemotherapy. Doctors can examine cancerous tissue during surgery to determine if it has spread and if further treatment is needed. Some surgeries cause permanent changes to the body. For example, people who have had a colostomy (partial removal of the colon) can no longer excrete waste as they normally would through the anus; rather, they excrete waste through an opening in their abdomen, which is then collected in a bag outside of the body.

5

BOMBARDING CANCER: RADIATION THERAPY

KEY POINTS

- Radiation therapy is used when surgery is risky or not feasible. It is also used in combination with other therapies: It can reduce a tumor prior to surgery; kill remaining cancer cells after surgery; be combined with chemotherapy; or reduce pain if the cancer is not treatable.

- Radiation also damages normal cells surrounding the cancerous tissue, and thus can cause certain side effects (fatigue, hair loss, nausea, vomiting), depending on the part of the body that's being treated.

- Radiation therapy can be in the form of external radiation, such as X-rays directed at the cancerous part of the body, or internal radiation, such as radiation "seeds" implanted in the cancerous organ.

About half of all cancer patients receive radiation therapy, either alone or with surgery or chemotherapy. Radiation therapy bombards cancer with X-rays, gamma rays, and subatomic particles (electrons, protons, and neutrons). Radiation therapy had its beginning when German scientist Wilhelm Röntgen discovered X-rays in 1895 (see box on page 68). X-rays are **electromagnetic radiation**, similar to the visible light that we can see (Figure 5.1). They have higher energy, however, and can penetrate into the body.

Radiation therapy is effective on cancer cells because they divide continually. Radiation damages DNA, and the DNA in continually dividing cells does not repair itself as well as the DNA in a normal cell, and damage accumulates. Eventually, the severely damaged DNA cannot reproduce itself, and the cancer cell dies while dividing. Radiation also damages cells in normal tissues, but fewer normal cells are damaged because they are dividing less frequently than cancer cells.

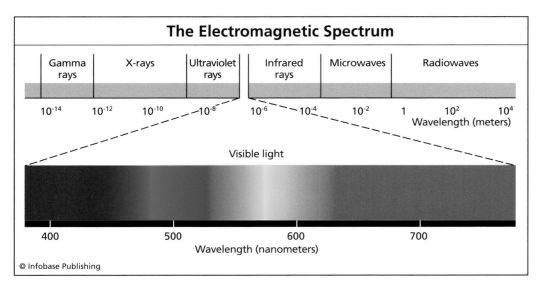

Figure 5.1 Visible light is only a small part of the electromagnetic spectrum. X-rays and gamma rays are high-energy forms of radiation and are used to treat cancer.

Radiation therapy is the main treatment for certain kinds of cancer of the **larynx** (voice box), lung, cervix, prostate, thyroid, and brain. Radiation therapy may be used instead of surgery if surgery is very risky or impossible. In some cases, surgery would completely remove an organ, while radiation therapy could spare the organ. For example, radiation therapy for cancer of the larynx instead of surgery to remove it can allow a patient to keep his or her voice.

In addition to being the main treatment used in some cases, radiation therapy is also used with other cancer therapies. It can shrink a tumor before surgery, making the surgery more successful. Used after surgery, it can kill cancer cells that the surgery may have left behind. Chemotherapy can be used with radiation therapy to kill cancer cells that may have spread from the original site. For cancers that are not treatable, radiation therapy can be used for palliation by shrinking tumors to relieve pain and other symptoms.

One limitation of radiation therapy is that it cannot destroy large tumors. The cancer cells in the center of a large tumor are supplied with less oxygen from blood than the cancer cells at the surface of the tumor. Because of this, the cells in the center do not divide rapidly, and many of them are not damaged by radiation therapy. Large tumors are treated with surgery alone, or with surgery and radiation therapy combined.

EXTERNAL RADIATION THERAPY

External radiation therapy directs X-rays or a beam of electrons from a machine called a linear accelerator into the body (Figure 5.3). The machine is called a linear accelerator because it accelerates a beam of electrons in a straight line either to smash into a target to produce X-rays or to travel directly into the tumor. Low-energy X-rays cannot penetrate

◆ THE DISCOVERY OF X-RAYS

X-rays are common in today's world and are used for everything from screening baggage at airports to making images of organs and bones inside the body. Because they are invisible, they were difficult to discover. In 1895 German scientist Wilhelm Röntgen was experimenting with a beam of electrons traveling inside a glass tube from one end to another. He was working in a dark room, and he noticed that a screen covered with a fluorescent material near the tube was glowing. This glowing seemed impossible because the tube was covered with cardboard and no light could escape from it. Excited by this mystery, he moved the screen farther and farther away until it was in another room. It still glowed. He experimented with his new discovery and found that whatever was coming from the tube could easily penetrate wood but was stopped by a thick piece of metal. He asked his wife, Bertha, to place her hand on a photographic plate near the tube, and found that the plate showed an image of the bones of her hand and her wedding ring. Röntgen correctly realized that he had discovered a new form of radiation and named his discovery "X-rays," with *X* standing for "unknown."

Today we know that X-rays are electromagnetic radiation just like visible light, but the eye cannot see them because their wavelength is too short. They can, however, make an image on film and on special screens. Röntgen's X-rays were produced when high-velocity electrons struck the sides of the glass tube. This is essentially the same way we produce X-rays today, more than a century later, except that the electrons now strike a metal target.

Because X-rays have high energy, they mostly pass through body tissues. But enough X-rays are blocked by the different types of tissue to form images that are useful for diagnosing medical conditions. Different

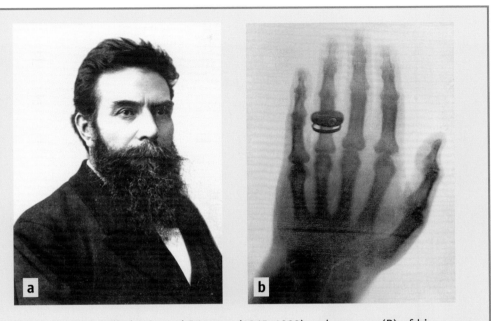

Figure 5.2 (A) Wilhelm Conrad Röntgen (1845–1923) and an x-ray (B) of his wife Bertha's hand. This is one of the first x-rays ever made. *(U.S. National Library of Medicine (A) and Bettman/CORBIS (B))*

tissues block X-rays to different degrees, with denser tissue like bone blocking the most and showing up as lighter areas on an X-ray image.

Röntgen's discovery caused a sensation within the scientific world and in the public. Within months X-rays were used for viewing broken bones, abnormal bone growth, and bullets and other objects embedded in the body. Within a few years, doctors began treating cancer with X-rays. They did not yet know about the damaging effects of radiation and they exposed themselves to massive doses of X-rays, causing skin burns, dying tissue, and cancer. Scientists began to understand more about the benefits and dangers of X-rays as the twentieth century went on. Today exposure to X-rays for both patients and medical staff is carefully controlled.

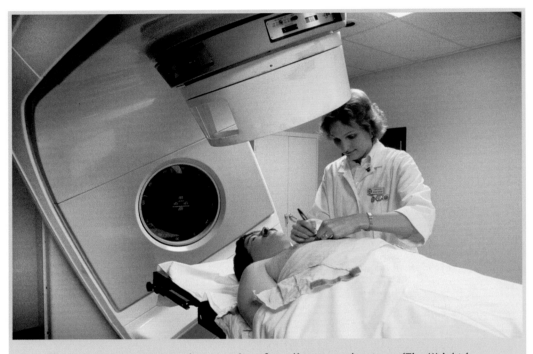

Figure 5.3 A nurse preparing a patient for a linear accelerator. *(Tim Wright/ CORBIS)*

very far into the body and are used mainly to treat skin cancer and other surface tumors. High-energy X-rays can reach deep into the body to bombard cancers in internal organs. Another type of electromagnetic radiation used in radiation therapy, called gamma rays, are like X-rays, but more energetic. A radioactive isotope like cobalt-60 gives them off. Less frequently, beams of protons or neutrons are used.

Newer technology makes external radiation therapy more effective. In stereotactic radiation therapy, a CT scan precisely maps the location of a brain cancer tumor. A computer calculates the amount of radiation needed and the directions from which it will come. An X-ray or gamma-ray machine uses this information to deliver doses of radiation to the tumor from different directions. This technique can hit the tumor with a large amount of radiation while causing less damage to the normal tissue surrounding it.

A radiation oncologist and a **medical physicist** carefully plan the dosage—amount—of radiation that the patient receives. They calculate the dose that is needed to destroy the tumor, then divide it into smaller doses that will be given five days a week for two to eight weeks. Spreading out the treatments delivers as much radiation to the tumor as possible without causing too much damage to normal tissue. Patients usually do not have to be hospitalized. They simply come in for their radiation therapy appointment and then leave when it is finished.

Because radiation therapy damages normal cells, it has side effects. The side effects depend on the part of the body that is being treated, the daily dose of radiation, and the total dose. Side effects vary with the individual patient. Some people experience almost no side effects, while others have severe problems. Fatigue is common because the body is healing itself, and many people will lose their appetite. The area being treated will lose hair, which may or may not grow back, depending on the dosage. The skin through which the radiation passes will temporarily become red, as if it is sunburned. If the patient is receiving radiation in the abdomen, nausea and vomiting may occur. If the patient is receiving radiation in the head or neck, the mucous membranes in the mouth and esophagus will become irritated and dry. Most side effects are temporary and will gradually go away once the therapy is finished.

Radiation may have long-term side effects, however. If radiation has been given to the pelvic area in women, they may have difficulty becoming pregnant because of damage to reproductive organs. Men can suffer from infertility after radiation treatment of the testicles. In rare cases radiation therapy can cause a new cancer (see box on page 73).

INTERNAL RADIATION THERAPY

In internal radiation therapy, radioactive isotopes of elements like iodine, gold, and cesium that produce electrons or gamma rays are inserted into or near the tumor. Internal radiation therapy usually causes less damage to normal tissue than external radiation therapy because the radiation source is placed inside or near the tumor, and higher doses can be used in a shorter period of time. Sometimes small "seeds"—about the size of a grain of rice—containing radioactive material are placed directly in the tumor. The seeds remain in the body permanently, gradually becoming less radioactive. In a method called interstitial radiation therapy, radiation oncologists first insert a plastic tube called an implant into the tumor. They then place the radioactive material in the implant. The implant is usually left in place for three to five days and then removed. In a similar method called intracavitary radiation therapy, the oncologist places a container in a hollow space, such as the uterus, then places the radioactive material in the container. In systemic radiation therapy, radioactive isotopes are injected into the body or swallowed, and are absorbed by the cancer cells. For example, the element iodine is normally taken up by the thyroid gland and used to make thyroid hormone. Radioactive iodine-131 is given to patients with thyroid cancer, and the cancer cells absorb the radioactive iodine and are destroyed.

The patient must stay in the hospital during internal radiation therapy and may need to remain in bed so that the implant or container stays in the proper place. During this time, the patient's body is continually

♦ CAN X-RAYS CAUSE CANCER?

There is no doubt that X-rays and other forms of radiation can cause cancer. Yet people routinely have diagnostic X-rays at visits to their dentist and doctor, and radiation therapy is prescribed for about half of all cancer patients. Is there a contradiction here?

We are all exposed to radiation from natural sources. This background radiation includes electromagnetic radiation and high-energy particles from the sun, from radioactive elements such as radon, and from cosmic rays coming from space. The background radiation that a person receives each year is greater than what a person receives from routine dental and medical X-rays. A routine X-ray is equivalent to a few days of background radiation. Nevertheless, low doses of radiation from any source do increase the risk of cancer very slightly; however, medical scientists believe that the benefits of routine X-rays outweigh the risk of cancer.

Radiation therapy involves much higher doses of radiation than routine X-rays, so is the risk of cancer greater? The answer is yes. Leukemia, breast cancer, lung cancer, and other cancers may occur 5, 10, or 20 years after radiation therapy has cured the original cancer. Although the risk of developing a secondary cancer from radiation therapy is difficult to measure, it appears to be low. Some cancer patients worry about radiation therapy giving them cancer. However, the risk of dying from cancer that is not treated is much greater than the risk of developing cancer from radiation therapy.

giving off a small amount of radiation. If the patient has been given systemic radiation therapy, fluids from the patient—such as urine and saliva—may contain the radioactive isotope. Radiation therapy nurses care for the patient, but work quickly and do not spend much time in the room to avoid exposing themselves to excessive amounts of radiation that they could get from tending to several radiation patients. They may also wear gloves and shoe covers, and use a portable radiation shield between themselves and the patient. Visitors may be told to stay six feet (1.8 m) away from the patient and limit their stay to 30 minutes. Children and pregnant women cannot visit.

BRIAN'S RADIATION THERAPY

Brian had had a sore throat off and on for months, and was now having difficulty swallowing food. He made an appointment with Dr. Delacy, his regular doctor. Dr. Delacy knew that Brian smoked tobacco and had been smoking for 30 years, which put him at a greatly increased risk for various types of mouth and throat cancers. During Brian's appointment, Dr. Delacy looked down Brian's throat with a small mirror and saw something suspicious in the larynx. The larynx, or voice box, is a 2-inch (5 cm) organ in the neck at the top of the windpipe that contains the vocal cords. When a person talks or sings, the vocal cords tighten, which causes them to vibrate as air moves through them. When a person breathes normally, the vocal cords are relaxed and air travels through the larynx and windpipe into the lungs without producing a sound.

Dr. Delacy referred Brian to Dr. Hoyer, an ear, nose, and throat specialist. Dr. Hoyer gave Brian an anesthetic to make him sleep and inserted a flexible endoscope called a laryngoscope down his throat. Dr. Hoyer saw an area in the larynx that looked like a tumor and took a biopsy sample to send to the laboratory. The pathologist examined the cells in the sample and determined that they were cancerous. He determined that they were grade 2. They looked slightly like normal larynx cells, but definitely had the abnormal characteristics of cancer cells. Dr. Hoyer ordered a CT scan to help determine the size of the cancer and whether it had spread from the larynx. The CT scan showed that the cancer was limited to the larynx, but it was large enough to include the vocal cords and the upper part of the larynx. It was judged to be a stage II cancer.

Laryngeal cancer accounts for about 10,000 new cases each year in the United States, about 1 percent of all cancers. It arises in the **squamous cells** that form the lining of the larynx. Men account for about 80 percent of laryngeal cancer cases because of their higher rates of smoking and excessive drinking compared to women. These two habits combined may increase the risk as much as 100 times compared to people without those habits. If not detected early, laryngeal cancer can spread to the lymph nodes in the neck, to other parts of the throat and neck, and to the lungs and liver.

Dr. Hoyer discussed possible treatments with Dr. Tofte, a surgical oncologist, and Dr. Warne, a radiation oncologist. One option was a partial laryngectomy, surgery to remove part of the larynx. This would affect Brian's voice, making it sound weak. Another option was external radiation therapy, either alone or combined with a partial laryngectomy. Dr. Hoyer and Brian discussed the treatment choices, and together they decided on radiation therapy without surgery, which would spare Brian's voice. If the cancer came back, however, then surgery would be necessary.

After Brian and Dr. Hoyer made the decision to use radiation therapy, Dr. Warne was put in charge of Brian's treatment. The first step in planning a treatment is called "simulation." A custom mask for Brian's head and neck was made out of plastic. Brian lay on his back wearing this mask, which was then attached to the radiotherapy table. He was careful not to move while a CT scan generated images of the tumor and surrounding tissue. These images were fed into a computer that uses special software to create three-dimensional images. Dr. Warne and a medical physicist examined these images to plan Brian's radiation therapy. They would use a newer technique called three-dimensional conformal radiation therapy (3-D CRT), which delivers beams of high-energy X-rays from different directions. The beams are precisely shaped to fit the tumor and minimize damage to nearby tissue, such as the spinal cord. Dr. Warne and the medical physicist determined the directions from which the radiation would enter the larynx, the shape of each beam of radiation, and the total amount of radiation Brian would receive. A radiation therapist then made small ink marks on Brian's neck to mark the treatment area. Dr. Warne and the medical physicist decided that Brian would receive one treatment a day, five days a week, for seven weeks.

Brian was understandably nervous when he went for his first treatment. After changing into a hospital gown, he entered the treatment room, put on his custom mask, and lay on the radiotherapy table. The radiation therapist attached the mask to the radiotherapy table and left the room. From her desk in an area shielded from the radiation, she turned on the 3-D CRT machine while watching Brian on closed-circuit television. A computer program containing the information for Brian's therapy controlled the machine. Brian kept very still as the machine moved around his body, whirring and clicking as it delivered X-rays to the tumor from different directions. Brian felt nothing. The session was over in 20 minutes, and Brian went home.

During the seven weeks of radiation therapy, Brian felt well enough to go to work on most days. Toward the end of treatment, he developed a sore throat and found that swallowing food was painful. Dr. Warne prescribed a painkiller, and Brian began a liquid diet. These side effects gradually went away after the therapy was finished. Radiation therapy has a 70 to 80 percent success rate in treating stage II laryngeal cancer like Brian's. He will be checked frequently during the coming years to monitor his health and to see if his cancer returns.

SUMMARY

Radiation therapy is effective in treating cancer because it damages the DNA of cancer cells to the point where it can no longer reproduce itself. Once bombarded by X-rays, gamma rays, or other forms of radiation, cancer cells stop dividing and die off. Radiation therapy can be done externally, with X-rays or a beam of electrons directed into the body, or internally, with radioactive isotopes inserted into or near the tumor. Certain kinds of cancer of the larynx, lung, cervix, prostate, thyroid, and brain are usually treated with radiation therapy.

6

CANCER-KILLING MOLECULES: CHEMOTHERAPY

KEY POINTS

- Chemotherapy consists of drugs taken either orally or through injections that are targeted to treat cancer. Unlike radiation therapy or surgery, chemotherapy treats the whole body and thus is used for widespread cancers.

- Chemotherapy interferes with the cancer cell's life cycle: it disrupts cell division and other processes and prevents cells from replicating.

- Many cancer drugs are from natural sources. For example, Taxol, one of the most frequently prescribed cancer drugs, is made of a compound found in certain yew trees.

Chemical warfare was used for the first time during World War I (1914–1918), and soldiers wearing gas masks are one of the most gripping images we have from that war. Mustard gas blistered the skin and lungs, and caused blindness and internal bleeding. An agonizing death could result, but it did not happen for several weeks. During and after the war, research on mustard gas and similar compounds showed that these chemicals destroyed bone marrow and lymphatic tissue. As part of the research on chemical warfare during World War II (1939–1945), scientists in the United States used nitrogen mustard, a chemical similar to mustard gas, to treat a terminal patient ill with lymphoma—cancer of the lymph nodes. The patient's tumors disappeared, and although they later returned, this experiment showed that chemicals could treat cancer. By investigating an agent of death, the door was opened to a new way of fighting cancer. More than 100 cancer drugs are in use today.

Most people with cancer will be treated with chemotherapy, either alone or combined with surgery or radiation therapy. Chemotherapy drugs are given by mouth or injected into a vein, and spread throughout the body in the bloodstream. Because chemotherapy treats the entire body, it can treat widespread cancers such as blood and bone marrow cancers, and cancer cells from tumors that have migrated to other sites. By contrast, surgery and most forms of radiation therapy deal with cancer at a specific site in the body. These therapies need to be supplemented with chemotherapy if cancer is suspected to have metastasized. Chemotherapy is the only treatment for some types of leukemia and lymphoma, which are not confined to one location in the body.

HOW CHEMOTHERAPY WORKS

Chemotherapy works by interrupting cell division and other cell processes during different phases of a cancer cell's life cycle: when DNA replicates itself, when the cell divides, and when the cell is carrying on its normal functions. **Alkylating agents** attach an **alkyl group** such

SPOTLIGHT ON CANCER SCIENTISTS
SIDNEY FARBER (1903-1973)

Until the second half of the twentieth century, children and adults with leukemia faced a certain death sentence. Leukemia is cancer of bone marrow cells in which abnormal cells are produced in huge numbers. Unlike cancers that form a tumor that can be surgically removed or killed with radiation, leukemia is found in bone marrow throughout the body. For the type of leukemia called acute lymphocytic leukemia, death could come within weeks after symptoms first appeared.

In 1947, Dr. Sidney Farber of Boston's Children's Hospital had an idea. He knew that folate, a vitamin, was needed to produce bone marrow cells, and reasoned that if he could find something that blocked folate, then the production of the abnormal bone marrow cells could be stopped. He obtained a chemical called aminopterin from a drug company. Aminopterin has a molecular structure similar to that of folate, and when aminopterin takes the place of folate in abnormal cells, the cells cannot reproduce.

Farber gave aminopterin to 16 children who were dying from acute lymphocytic leukemia. The leukemia in 10 of the children improved

as a methyl group (CH_3) to a cancer cell's DNA during any phase of the cell's life cycle. The cell tries to repair the DNA damage using special proteins called **repair enzymes**, but instead, the enzymes break the DNA apart. Alternatively, an alkylating agent such as cyclophosphamide has an alkyl group that attaches itself to two DNA molecules. The DNA molecules are then linked together and cannot replicate themselves.

temporarily. Farber and others continued to work on the problem and soon found that a similar chemical, methotrexate, was more effective. Sixty years later, methotrexate is still used to treat many cancers.

Although Farber's initial work with children would be called a failure by today's standards, it was an important advance at that time because chemotherapy was just beginning. For the first time, doctors and scientists saw a ray of hope that leukemia could be cured, and also saw a new way of doing drug research. Previously, a large number of chemicals would be tested

Figure 6.1 Sidney Farber. *(U.S. National Library of Medicine)*

in hopes of finding one that works, or a scientist would stumble upon an effective drug by accident. Farber's work is one of the first examples of rational drug design, in which a drug is designed to target a specific molecule in a cancer cell.

Antimetabolites mimic natural metabolites (chemicals that are essential for life) and interfere with a cancer cell's normal processes, including those needed for DNA replication. For example, the drug methotrexate is similar to folate, a vitamin that is necessary for DNA replication in all cells. Folate attaches itself to a protein to form an enzyme, a type of protein that speeds up chemical reactions in cells.

The enzyme, in turn, produces the molecules needed to make DNA. When methotrexate—instead of folate—attaches itself to the protein, the resulting molecule cannot function as an enzyme and DNA replication is stopped.

Chemotherapy drugs have many other ways to kill cancer cells. Drugs made with the element platinum cause two DNA molecules to link to one another, like alkylating agents do. **Mitotic inhibitors** stop the division of the cell nucleus (mitosis). **Antitumor antibiotics** bind to DNA, which prevents RNA from being produced. A tumor must develop new blood vessels to feed itself, a process called angiogenesis.

♦ THE CURE FROM A TREE

In 1962, Arthur Barclay of the U.S. Department of Agriculture gathered bark and needles from Pacific yew trees (*Taxus brevifolia*) in Washington State as part of a National Cancer Institute effort to find anticancer compounds in plants. As part of the same project, Monroe Wall and Mansukh Wani of the Research Triangle Institute in North Carolina were isolating promising compounds from plants. Barclay's yew samples were sent to Wall and Wani's laboratory, and in 1967 they isolated a compound, paclitaxel, that showed antitumor effects in mice.

But a large obstacle was in the way. A mature Pacific yew tree, which might be 200 years old, produced only 0.02 oz (0.5 grams) of paclitaxel. It would take several Pacific yew trees, which are not common, to provide enough of the compound to treat just one patient. Environmentalists objected to the possibility of devastating the population of these trees. Fortunately, researchers found that the more common English yew tree

Antiangiogenesis drugs are being studied that prevent new blood vessels from forming in tumors. New chemotherapy techniques being tested include **liposomal therapy**, in which drugs are placed inside liposomes (artificial fat globules) that penetrate cancer cells more readily than normal cells, and thus reduce the side effects.

Certain glands produce chemical messengers called hormones that circulate throughout the body and control cells and organs. Hormone therapy uses our knowledge of how hormones work to control certain cancers. In women, the ovaries produce estrogen, the female sex hormone that causes the development of the breasts, ovaries, and uterus,

(*Taxus baccata*) contained a large amount of a similar compound that could be converted into paclitaxel.

Testing on human patients in the 1980s showed that paclitaxel was effective in treating cancer of the ovaries. In the 1990s the Food and Drug Administration (FDA) approved paclitaxel for cancer of the ovaries, breast cancer, and Kaposi's sarcoma. Today paclitaxel, better known by its brand name, Taxol®, is one of the most frequently prescribed cancer drugs.

Paclitaxel's origin is not unique among cancer drugs. Many other cancer drugs come from natural sources. Daunorubicin was first isolated from a soil bacteria, *Streptomyces coeruleorubidus*. Vincristine was first isolated from the leaves of a periwinkle plant. These drugs and many others show that despite our ability to create compounds at will in the laboratory, we still rely on nature to point the way to compounds that may be effective against cancer and other diseases. And we have just begun to search for them: Scientists have examined only a small percentage of the 300,000 plants on Earth.

and controls the menstrual cycle. The estrogen molecule stimulates cells to grow and divide by attaching to a protein in the cell called a hormone receptor. Cancer cells, as well as normal cells, in the breast respond to estrogen, and hormone therapy for breast cancer involves blocking this estrogen response. A drug called tamoxifen binds to the hormone receptors and prevents estrogen from binding. In males, the testes produce **testosterone**, the male sex hormone that causes the development of the male reproductive organs. Testosterone stimulates prostate cancer cells to grow and divide. Antiandrogen (androgen is a general term for male sex hormones) drugs such as flutamide bind to the hormone receptors and prevent testosterone from binding.

CHEMOTHERAPY SIDE EFFECTS

There is no getting around it: Chemotherapy uses brutally harsh chemicals that affect cells in normal tissues, not just cancer cells. Chemotherapy is particularly hard on cells that divide rapidly, such as those in the bone marrow, hair follicles, mouth, stomach, and intestines. Some chemotherapy drugs can damage organs like the heart, lungs, kidneys, liver, ovaries, and testes. The side effects vary widely, depending on the type of drug and the individual patient.

Of special concern is the effect of chemotherapy on bone marrow, which produces several types of blood cells, including white and red blood cells and **platelets**. White blood cells fight infection, and low levels of these cells (leukopenia) during chemotherapy can lead to a serious infection, particularly because chemotherapy can also suppress the immune system. Red blood cells carry oxygen, and low levels of these cells (**anemia**) can cause fatigue. Platelets stop bleeding, and low levels of these (thrombocytopenia) can lead to internal bleeding and excessive bleeding from small cuts. The amounts of these cells in the blood are monitored carefully during chemotherapy that involves bone marrow. The levels are expected to go down, but if the level of any of these three types of blood cells falls dangerously low, chemotherapy can be stopped temporarily or the dose of the drug lowered. The patient may also receive blood cell transfusions.

Nausea, vomiting, and diarrhea are also common side effects after a chemotherapy treatment and may last for days. The doctor may prescribe medications to relieve these symptoms. Other side effects that may develop over the course of treatment include weight loss, hair loss, and sores in the mouth.

Because most chemotherapy drugs act on DNA, they produce mutations in normal cells. In rare cases some of these mutations lead to cancer. Like radiation therapy, chemotherapy has a slight risk of causing a new cancer while curing the current one. Alkylating agents in particular have been shown to cause cancer, with leukemia being the most common. As with radiation therapy, however, the risk of not using chemotherapy is much greater than the risk of developing another cancer.

PLANNING

Because each cancer and each patient is different, the medical oncologist plans the chemotherapy for the individual patient. Two to five drugs are usually given in a certain sequence to attack the cancer cells at different phases of their life cycle. In addition, a combination of drugs reduces the chance that the cancer will develop a resistanc—the ability to survive a drug treatment. A cancer can develop a resistance to a particular drug because cancer cells in a tumor are constantly mutating and are not identical to one another. The cancer cells that are sensitive to the drug are killed, but other cancer cells are resistant, and they survive and divide. The tumor may initially shrink, but then grow again because the resistant cells continue to divide. In other words the drug actually selects the resistant cells for further reproduction. The tumor is now resistant to the drug. A combination of drugs is used because it is much less likely that the original cancer cells will be resistant to several different drugs.

Chemotherapy drugs are very powerful, and there is frequently little difference between a dose that is effective in killing the cancer and a dose that is toxic to the patient. There are no firm rules about what a proper dose should be. The medical oncologist determines the dosage of each drug for a particular patient by considering several factors: the stage of the cancer, the patient's body weight, the general health of the patient, other drugs the patient is taking, whether the patient has had radiation therapy, and whether the patient has abnormalities of the blood, liver, or kidneys. The dosage may have to be reduced during treatment if the patient develops serious side effects.

TREATMENT

Chemotherapy is usually given in cycles in which the drugs are administered and then the body is allowed to recover. The idea is to kill off most of the cancer cells in each cycle, with fewer and fewer cancer cells remaining to attack during the next cycle. The cycles vary widely, from administering the chemotherapy one day a month to as often as five days in a row every week. For example, a patient may be on a three-week cycle in which drug #1 is given on day 1 and day 5; drug #2 is given on days 1, 7, and 13; and drug #3 is given on days 5, 10, and 15. No drugs are given on days 16 through 21, to allow the body time to recover. The cycles may continue for six months to a year.

If a chemotherapy drug is absorbed by the digestive system, it can be given by mouth. Most drugs, however, are delivered directly into the bloodstream by one of several methods. The oncology nurse can inject the drug into a vein in the forearm or hand with a needle, either with a syringe or as a slow drip from a bag of fluid that contains the drug. Injection into veins can be a problem because a patient's veins can become scarred or even collapse after repeated needle sticks during cycles of chemotherapy.

One alternative is to insert a narrow plastic catheter—a hollow, flexible tube—into a large vein. Part of the catheter sticks out of the skin and has a thin rubber cap that a needle can easily pass through. The catheter is left in place for many treatments and is not painful to the patient. The oncology nurse injects the drug into the catheter without having to stick the patient with a needle. The catheter can also be used to administer antinausea drugs, painkillers, nutrients, and **antibiotics**. A catheter needs some maintenance. It should be kept clean and the rubber cap needs to be changed periodically. A drug called heparin is injected to prevent blood from clotting in the catheter.

Another alternative that does not require as much care is a type of catheter called a port that is inserted completely under the skin during minor surgery. The oncology nurse then injects the drug through the skin and the rubber cap into the catheter.

If the cancer is localized the drug is sometimes delivered directly to the tumor instead of through a vein that may be far away from the cancer site. Liver cancer can be treated by injecting the drug slowly with a special pump into an artery that carries blood into the liver. Ovarian cancer can be treated by injecting the drug through a catheter into the abdominal cavity.

If the drug-delivery method is slow or if the drug has serious side effects, the patient may stay in the hospital for a day or longer. Some drugs may be given during a short visit to the oncologist's office, after which the patient will return home or to work if he or she is feeling well enough.

As the treatment progresses, the oncologist monitors the cancer's response to the chemotherapy. He or she uses one or more of the diagnostic procedures that originally detected the cancer, such as blood tests, imaging techniques like CT scans, and tumor markers (see Chapter 2).

MATTHEW'S CHEMOTHERAPY

Matthew was a normal, energetic seven-year-old boy until he began complaining about feeling tired and having pain in his shoulders and ribs. His mother became alarmed when he returned from soccer practice with several dark bruises and scrapes that would not stop bleeding. She immediately took him to his doctor, Dr. Henderson. The symptoms worried Dr. Henderson, and she had a nurse take a blood sample from Matthew and immediately send it to the lab so that a **blood cell count** could be done. The count showed that Matthew's red blood cells and platelets were dangerously low, and his white blood cells were very high. Furthermore, most of the white blood cells did not look like normal cells.

Dr. Henderson suspected the worst: leukemia. Because leukemia can cause death within weeks or even days of the first symptoms, she immediately sent Matthew and his mother to Lowery General Hospital, which has a **pediatric** cancer center. There, a doctor gave Matthew an injection of a xylocaine, a local anesthetic, and inserted a needle into his hipbone to withdraw a sample of bone marrow. The doctor then sent the marrow sample to the laboratory for diagnosis.

The lab results came back the next day and showed that Matthew had leukemia—cancer of the bone marrow. Further tests showed that it was **acute lymphocytic leukemia**—*acute* means that the disease will progress quickly (Figure 6.2).

Matthew returned to the hospital that day with his parents. The doctor had Matthew lie on his side and then performed a spinal tap: after injecting xylocaine, the doctor inserted a needle into Matthew's

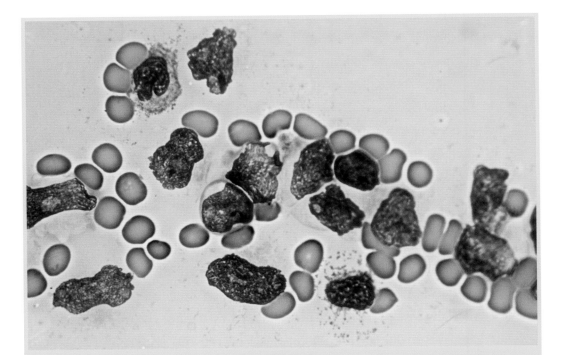

Figure 6.2 In acute lymphocytic leukemia, immature stem cells rapidly multiply and crowd out other stem cells, preventing them from producing normal blood cells. (*Biology Media/Photo Researchers, Inc.*)

lower spine between two vertebrae and withdrew a sample of **cerebrospinal fluid**. Laboratory analysis brought back good news: the leukemia had not spread to Matthew's central nervous system—the brain and spinal cord.

In normal bone marrow, undeveloped cells called **stem cells** gradually mature into red blood cells, white blood cells, and platelets. Some stem cells mature into a type of white blood cell called **lymphocytes**. In acute lymphocytic leukemia these stem cells remain immature and multiply continually. The leukemic cells fill up the bone marrow, crowding out normal stem cells and preventing the production of normal red and white blood cells and platelets. They spill out into the blood and lymphatic system, and invade the brain and spinal cord. Acute lymphocytic leukemia is the most common cancer in children, accounting for about one-third of all childhood cancers—about 2,000 new cases a year in the United States. It is most common in children two to three years old. Fortunately cancer of any type is rare in children, amounting to less than 1 percent of the number of cancers in adults.

Matthew and his parents were immediately taken to Dr. Connley, a pediatric oncologist at the hospital. Dr. Connley explained to Matthew's parents that chemotherapy needed to begin immediately, that same day. Matthew would be given a combination of drugs and then checked to see how they affected the leukemia. If all went well, remission would happen quickly, in a few weeks. Nonetheless chemotherapy would continue for as long as three years to prevent the leukemia from returning.

Matthew was afraid of what was happening to him. The procedures that had been done were painful, and he did not understand why they had to be done. His parents were even more frightened. They understood what leukemia was and they knew there was a possibility that Matthew could die. They also knew that Matthew would need to undergo a long period of chemotherapy that would have serious and unpleasant side effects.

In preparation for his chemotherapy, Matthew was put under general anesthesia and a surgeon inserted a catheter into a large vein above the heart in his chest. The surgeon threaded the catheter through the vein until the end was at the entrance to the **right atrial chamber** of the heart (Figure 6.3). The catheter would remain in place for many treatments so that the drugs could be given and blood samples withdrawn without new painful needle sticks.

Matthew would remain in the hospital most of the time through the first phase of treatment, called induction, which lasted four weeks. Induction is designed to achieve remission, which, in the case of acute lymphocytic leukemia, means that the bone marrow no longer contains leukemic cells, the normal marrow stem cells are returning, and the blood cell count is normal. The oncology nurse administered three drugs to Matthew during the induction phase: vincristine (once a week) and asparaginase (every third day) through the catheter, and daily doses of dexamethasone by mouth. In addition to the drugs administered through the catheter, Dr. Connley injected methotrexate into the lower part of Matthew's spine as a precaution to kill leukemic cells that may have spread to the central nervous system, even though the laboratory tests did not show any leukemia there.

The first few doses of the chemotherapy drugs did not affect Matthew. After that, however, he became nauseated and vomited frequently. Chemotherapy doesn't kill just the leukemic cells in the bone marrow; normal stem cells are also killed. Because his white blood cells were depleted, Matthew developed a fever from an infection and was given

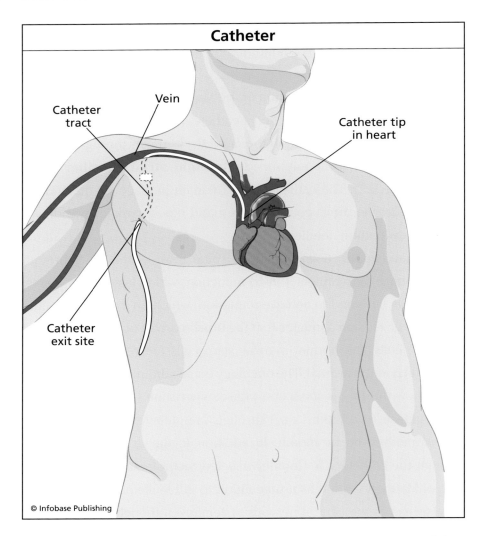

Figure 6.3 A catheter inserted through a vein and run up to the entrance of the heart. The catheter will remain in place and chemotherapy drugs can be given through the catheter, and blood samples taken, without repeated needle sticks.

an antibiotic. His red blood cell count became low and he was given a transfusion of red blood cells. His hair began to fall out, and he would lose almost all of it over the next few weeks.

One of Matthew's parents stayed with him at the hospital all the time, keeping him entertained by reading to him and playing board games. His teacher sent schoolwork to the hospital so Matthew would not fall too far behind. Although he frequently felt tired and sick, he worked on his schoolwork with his parents.

Dr. Connley took a bone marrow sample on day seven, and the laboratory found few leukemic cells present. Matthew's blood had been checked daily, and no leukemic cells were found on this day. These results showed that the chemotherapy was working. Over the next three weeks, Matthew's marrow stem cells gradually returned and his blood count started to look normal.

After one month Dr. Connley decided that Matthew's leukemia was in remission, and Matthew could return to school on days when he felt well. This did not mean that all the leukemic cells were gone. There may be several million cells remaining out of about 100 billion at the start of chemotherapy, and these cells would still have to be killed. Matthew's chemotherapy moved to the next phase, consolidation, which would last six months. During this phase, Matthew would return to the hospital every two weeks so that the oncology nurse could administer methotrexate, mercaptopurine, and vincristine through his catheter.

After the consolidation phase was complete, the maintenance phase began, and Matthew started taking lower doses of methotrexate (weekly) and mercaptopurine (daily) by mouth. This phase lasted two years.

This was a traumatic time in the lives of Matthew and his parents, but it could have been worse—he could have died. The leukemia did not return during the two and a half years of treatment, and Matthew has an 80 percent chance of being permanently cured.

SUMMARY

Chemotherapy is the use of strong drugs that interfere with the life cycle of cancer cells. The drugs can be taken by mouth or through injections, and they have different ways of killing cancer: They can interfere with DNA replicating itself, they can stop cell division, and they can interfere with processes necessary for the cancer cell to live. Chemotherapy also kills normal cells, and thus can cause serious side effects (depending on the type of drug and the individual being treated). These side effects can include nausea, vomiting, diarrhea, and organ and bone marrow damage.

7

STEM CELL TRANSPLANT
AND BIOLOGICAL THERAPY

KEY POINTS

- Our immune system (a system of organs and cells) protects us from foreign organisms and substances. It usually recognizes mutated proteins on the surface of cancer cells as antigens and destroys the cancer cells. But sometimes, because the cancer cells are our own cells, it will not attack them.

- Stem cell transplant and other biological therapies use the body's immune system to fight cancer. Stem cell transplant is the donation of a healthy person's stem cells to the cancer patient, so that the new stem cells can produce white blood cells that might destroy the cancer cells.

- Biological therapy is the use of certain proteins to help the immune system attack cancer cells.

Our bodies are invaded by millions of bacteria, viruses, and fungi each day. We breathe them in, swallow them, and absorb them through tiny cuts in our skin. Fortunately, almost all of them are harmless. Some, however, can cause serious illness and even death. What protects us is the **immune system**, a network of organs and cells that recognize and attack foreign organisms and substances. The cells in the immune system recognize **antigens**—the protein or carbohydrate molecules on the surface of the foreign invaders—as being different from the molecules on the surface of the body's cells. Seeing this difference is the signal to attack and destroy the invaders.

Hematopoietic stem cells (*hema* means "blood" and *poietic* means "forming") in the bone marrow produce all the white blood cells, red blood cells, and platelets in the body. Lymphocytes and **phagocytes**, two types of white blood cells, are the main parts of the immune system. Lymphocytes include **B cells**, **T cells**, and **natural killer cells**.

In addition to the bone marrow, the immune system includes the thymus, lymph nodes, and spleen (Figure 7.1). Stem cells develop into mature B cells in the bone marrow, but immature T cells produced in the bone marrow develop into mature T cells in the thymus, a small organ in the top of the chest. Lymph nodes are small, bean-shaped organs found in the neck, chest, groin, and other parts of the body. Lymphocytes concentrate in lymph nodes, where they attack the foreign invaders that have been brought there by the body's circulatory system. The spleen is a fist-sized organ on the left side of the body near the stomach. It is a complex organ that filters out and breaks down old blood cells and houses the phagocytes that attack foreign invaders in the blood.

The antigens on the surface of foreign invaders stimulate the B cells to produce proteins called antibodies that attach themselves to the

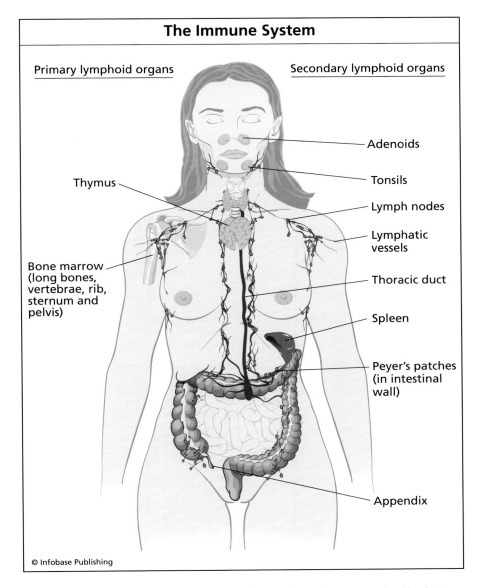

The Immune System

Primary lymphoid organs

Secondary lymphoid organs

Adenoids

Tonsils

Thymus

Lymph nodes

Lymphatic vessels

Bone marrow (long bones, vertebrae, rib, sternum and pelvis)

Thoracic duct

Spleen

Peyer's patches (in intestinal wall)

Appendix

© Infobase Publishing

Figure 7.1 The immune system is a complex system of organs and cells that protect your body from bacteria, viruses, and fungi. The primary organs are the bone marrow and thymus. Secondary organs are the tonsils, spleen, lymph nodes, and appendix.

◆ IMMUNE SYSTEM DESTROYER

A puzzling new disease seemed to come out of nowhere in 1981. Apparently healthy young homosexual men in the United States were being diagnosed with two rare diseases: pneumonia caused by the fungus *Pneumocystis carinii* and a cancer called Kaposi's sarcoma. It soon became obvious that these and other young homosexual men were contracting diseases that people get when their immune system is not functioning. As more and more cases appeared, the Centers for Disease Control and Prevention (CDC) began an effort to find the cause.

The disease acquired a name in 1982: acquired immune deficiency syndrome (AIDS). The vagueness of the name shows how little scientists knew about it: It affected the immune system, it was acquired rather than inherited, and it was a syndrome—a group of symptoms—rather than a well-defined disease. The cause was unknown. At first, it seemed to spread only through homosexual sex and intravenous drug use, but by 1983, it was obvious that it also spread through heterosexual sex and blood transfusions.

In 1983, American Robert Gallo and Frenchman Luc Montagnier independently isolated the virus that causes AIDS from a patient. It was named human immunodeficiency virus (HIV). Further research showed that HIV destroys T cells, which are responsible for attacking bacteria and viruses that invade the body and cancer cells that develop within it. Without T cells, all sorts of common and rare infections can spread unchecked through the body, causing serious illness and death.

As the years passed, the number of cases went from hundreds to thousands to millions. By 2005, 40.3 million people around the world were infected with HIV. The vast majority of HIV-infected people are in Africa, with a little over one million in the United States. Although drugs can control AIDS, they cannot cure it. Death will eventually occur, even if it is delayed for many years. Furthermore, the HIV virus mutates rapidly, producing strains of the virus that are resistant to current drugs. The rapid mutation of the virus also means that scientists who are trying to develop an AIDS vaccine have a tough time. Vaccines are designed to recognize specific molecules called antigens in viruses and bacteria, and the antigens in HIV viruses are continually changing.

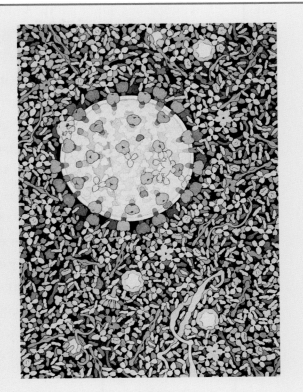

Figure 7.2 Human Immunodeficiency Virus (round pink cell) in blood. HIV causes AIDS by destroying the body's T cells. The body is then defenseless against many types of infections. (*David Goodsell/Photo Researchers, Inc.*)

The rise of AIDS was shocking to the medical community and the general population. We had eliminated or greatly controlled many diseases like smallpox, tuberculosis, and pneumonia, and were perhaps overconfident about being able to cure any disease. But here was a disease that resisted our best efforts—and continues to do so. Despite the gloomy outlook for a cure, there is one sure-fire way of combating AIDS: prevention. The virus does not spread easily, and avoiding unprotected sex and intravenous drug use provides virtually 100 percent protection.

antigens. The antibodies either kill the invaders directly or mark them for attack by other cells of the immune system. T cells attack the invaders and also release proteins called **cytokines** that call other immune cells into action. Phagocytes literally engulf the invaders. Natural killer cells attack cells that are infected with viruses.

Cancer cells are produced frequently in everyone's body, but the immune system usually recognizes the mutated proteins on the surface of cancer cells as antigens and destroys the cancer cells. However, cancer cells are the body's own cells, and sometimes they are so similar to normal cells that the immune system does not attack them. The dream of scientists is to get the immune system to always treat cancer cells as foreign and attack them before they can form a tumor. In recent decades, medical researchers have developed stem cell transplants and biological therapies that use the body's immune system to fight cancer. These therapies are now taking their place alongside the big three treatments—surgery, radiation therapy, and chemotherapy.

STEM CELL TRANSPLANTS

Bone marrow stem cell transplants have been used to treat certain cancers, mainly some types of leukemia and lymphoma, since the 1960s. One use for stem cell transplants is to support chemotherapy or radiation therapy. Stem cells, like cancer cells, are more susceptible to chemotherapy or radiation than other tissue cells because they divide continually. A dose of chemotherapy drugs or radiation may not be high enough to be effective against the cancer, unless it is increased to the point that it kills all the patient's stem cells. Killing the stem cells would normally be fatal because the patient could no longer produce new blood cells, but higher doses of drugs or radiation can be used, even if they kill the patient's original stem cells, because they can be replaced by transplanted stem cells.

A stem cell transplant from another person can also kill cancer cells directly. A patient's own white blood cells may not recognize cancer cells as foreign, but white blood cells produced by stem cells from another person are different. These white blood cells are from the immune system of another person and might destroy the cancer cells. The transplant procedure first uses radiation or chemotherapy to deliberately destroy the patient's stem cells, since these stem cells were ineffective against cancer or were maybe even the *source* of the cancer, as in leukemia. Next, stem cells from another person are transplanted to the patient.

A patient can receive one of three types of bone marrow stem cell transplants. In an autologous transplant, a doctor removes stem cells from the patient and freezes them. The patient then receives high-dose chemotherapy or radiation therapy to kill the cancer cells. The stem cells remaining in the body are also probably destroyed. The stored stem cells are then returned to the patient. One danger of autologous transplants is that the transplanted stem cells might still contain cancer cells.

In an allogeneic transplant, the patient also receives high-dose chemotherapy or radiation therapy to kill the cancer and the stem cells remaining in his body. The patient then receives the stem cells from a brother or sister that have been matched to the patient's own stem cells. A brother or sister has a 25 percent chance of providing a match. Less frequently another relative or an unrelated person can be the donor. In a syngeneic transplant, the patient receives stem cells from an identical twin—a perfect match.

How is the patient matched with a donor for an allogeneic transplant? Human leukocyte antigens (HLAs) are proteins found on the surface of nearly all cells in the body. The immune system uses these proteins to recognize "self" (the body) from "non-self" (foreign invaders). There are many HLAs, and different people have different combinations of them. The patient's HLAs and the potential donor's HLAs are identified by a special test. The greater the number of HLAs that a donor and patient have in common, the better the chance of a successful transplant.

When an allogeneic stem cell transplant is designed to kill cancer cells rather than support chemotherapy or radiation therapy, it relies on the graft-versus-tumor effect: The new white blood cells produced by the donor's stem cells (the graft) recognize the cancer cells as foreign to the body and kill them. But allogeneic transplants are a double-edged sword. The body may reject the donated stem cells, leaving the patient unable to produce any blood cells. In addition, the white blood cells produced by the donated stem cells may identify the patient's normal cells as foreign and attack them, an effect known as graft-versus-host disease. The disease most commonly attacks cells in the skin, liver, and intestines. Medications are given after the transplant to reduce the chance of graft-versus-host disease.

In an older procedure, which is still being used, doctors insert a large needle into the hip bone of a donor to remove 0.5 to 1 quart (500 to 1,000 milliliters) of bone marrow. The donor is given a general or regional anesthesia, and the procedure takes about an hour. One hundred to several hundred needle punctures are needed to withdraw enough marrow for a transplant. The donor's marrow will replenish itself over the next few weeks. The donated marrow is processed to remove blood and pieces of bone, and can be frozen if not needed immediately. The marrow is given to the patient intravenously, like a blood transfusion. The stem cells in the donated marrow migrate to the patient's bones and begin producing blood cells over a period of weeks.

A process that harvests stem cells from the blood, which is simpler and less painful, is rapidly replacing the bone marrow stem cell transplant procedure. A small quantity of stem cells circulate in the blood—too few to be useful in transplants. However, the donor can be given a drug for a few days before the transplant that causes the bone marrow to release large numbers of stem cells into the bloodstream. Blood is then removed from a large vein in the donor's arm, neck, or chest, and passed through a machine that removes the stem cells and returns the blood to the donor. This procedure takes about five hours.

Stem cell transplants are a high-risk procedure, and are usually done only after a standard treatment fails. Chemotherapy and radiation destroys the bone marrow, so the patient temporarily lacks the ability to produce white blood cells, red blood cells, and platelets. Because the concentrations of these cells in the blood drop below normal, infection, bleeding, and anemia are dangers in all types of stem cell transplants. The patient may spend several weeks in a special hospital room with filtered air to reduce the chance of bacteria and viruses entering the body and may be given antibiotics and transfusions of platelets and red blood cells. Less serious side effects include nausea, vomiting, fatigue, and loss of appetite

BIOLOGICAL THERAPIES

Biological therapies use certain proteins to activate the immune system and help it attack cancer cells. In developing new biological therapies, scientists hope to find ways to attack cancer cells specifically, as opposed to radiation and chemotherapy, which also damage normal cells.

Naturally occurring cytokines that are released by cells of the immune system can be manufactured in laboratories and used in cancer therapy. Interferons help the immune system attack cancer cells and also slow their growth and cause them to develop into more normal cells. Interleukins stimulate the growth of lymphocytes, a major part of the immune system, and help them recognize cancer cells. Interleukins are used to treat kidney cancer and melanoma.

Colony-stimulating factors increase the number of white blood cells produced by the bone marrow. Chemotherapy damages bone marrow, and by using colony-stimulating factors to stimulate extra white blood cell production, a higher dose of chemotherapy drugs can be given. The extra white blood cells help the patient avoid infection during chemotherapy.

Monoclonal antibodies recognize specific cancer cells. To manufacture them, cancer cells are injected into mice (Figure 7.3). The B cells in the mice's immune systems then produce antibodies that attack the cancer cells. The next step is surprising: Scientists collect the mice's B cells and fuse them with human bone marrow cancer cells! The reason this technique works is that cancer cells are immortal, and the combination of the two cells—a hybrid—is a cell that can grow, divide, and produce antibodies forever in the laboratory. A single hybrid cell is isolated and made to divide many times to produce a large colony of cells. All of the cells are clones—identical copies—of the original cell, which leads to the term *monoclonal* (*mono* means "one"). The hybrid cell produces antibodies that link up with the antigens on the type of cancer cells injected into the mice. The antibodies directly destroy these types of cancer cells in patients, or allow the cancer cells to be detected and destroyed by the body's immune system. The antibodies will not attack other cells. The antibodies can also be linked to radioactive isotopes or chemotherapy drugs and will carry them to the cancer cell. Monoclonal

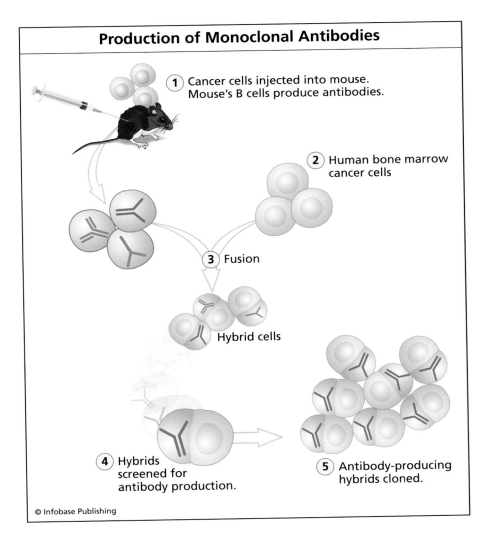

Production of Monoclonal Antibodies

1. Cancer cells injected into mouse. Mouse's B cells produce antibodies.

2. Human bone marrow cancer cells

3. Fusion

Hybrid cells

4. Hybrids screened for antibody production.

5. Antibody-producing hybrids cloned.

© Infobase Publishing

Figure 7.3 Scientists produce monoclonal antibodies by first injecting cancer cells into mice. The B cells in the mice's immune system produce antibodies to attack the cancer cells. Scientists then fuse the B cells with human bone marrow cancer cells. These new cells multiply rapidly and produce large quantities of antibodies that are used to fight the type of cancer cells that were originally injected into the mice.

antibodies are used to treat non-Hodgkin's lymphoma, breast cancer, and several other types of cancer.

The proteins used in different biological therapies are injected into a muscle or a vein. Fever, fatigue, chills, and swelling at the injection site are common and are sometimes severe. More serious side effects include a drop in blood pressure and **anaphylaxis**, a severe allergic reaction. Patients undergoing interleukin therapy are sometimes kept in the hospital during therapy because of possible life-threatening side effects.

CLINICAL TRIALS OF NEW THERAPIES

One key weapon against cancer is the human factor: Many cancer patients are willing to volunteer to test new therapies in **clinical trials**. Clinical trials investigate new surgical techniques, chemotherapy drugs, radiation therapy techniques, biological therapies, and combinations of different therapies. Scientists experiment with new therapies in animals before deciding whether it is promising enough to start the three phases of clinical trials in humans.

A phase I clinical trial involves 10 to 20 patients to investigate the best way to administer the new therapy and to determine whether it is safe and shows at least some effect on the cancer. The benefit to the patient is uncertain because this is the first step in testing a new therapy. The patients who take part in these tests usually have advanced cancer that has not responded to other therapies, and so they may reason that they have nothing to lose. Some patients may also want to help cancer research.

A phase II clinical trial involves 20 to 100 patients to determine if the new therapy has enough effect on cancer to advance to a phase III clinical trial. This process may take about two years, during which the responses of the patients' cancers are compared to a standard therapy that is commonly used for patients with this type of cancer.

A phase III clinical trial is the final study of the new therapy. It takes about three years. It is a massive effort. The hundreds—or thousands—of patients in the trial are divided into two groups: One group receives a standard therapy while the other group receives the new therapy. Patients do not know which therapy they are receiving. If the new therapy appears to be more effective than the standard therapy while the trial is still under way, the trial is stopped and all patients begin receiving the new therapy. If the trial is successful, the Food and Drug Administration (FDA) will approve the new therapy for use by all doctors.

Although the benefits are uncertain, cancer patients may decide to participate in clinical trials, with most of the benefits coming from being part of a phase III trial. Patients may benefit if the new therapy is better than the standard therapy. They will be monitored more carefully than other cancer patients usually are. However, clinical trials have disadvantages. Patients may receive the standard therapy instead of the new therapy that they hoped to receive. In addition, the new therapy may not be as effective as the standard therapy, and the patient may experience unexpected side effects. Despite these disadvantages, many cancer patients volunteer because they want to help improve cancer therapy for all cancer patients.

Clinical research is a massive effort, with $3.5 billion a year being invested in basic research and clinical trials. About 100 drugs are currently in phase III clinical trials, and more are in the pipeline leading up to this last phase.

THE FUTURE OF BIOLOGICAL THERAPIES

Newspaper headlines frequently report a successful new biological therapy or a promising advance in research. For example, in 2005, doctors reported that a vaccine for human papillomavirus (HPV) prevents infection by that virus, which can cause cancer of the cervix. Another promising area is gene therapy, in which missing or defective genes that can cause cancer are replaced with normal genes. Surprisingly, in gene therapy, a virus is actually used to deliver the genes to the cells' DNA. In a different approach, a virus is designed so that it will infect only a specific type of cancer cell. Once in the cancer cell, the virus reproduces itself rapidly, and the thousands of new viruses cause the cancer cell to burst open and die.

Biological therapies are relatively new and are considered to be in an early phase of development. So far each biological therapy is effective against one or a few kinds of cancer—fewer than the number of cancers that are treated by surgery, radiation therapy, and chemotherapy. Scientists do not believe that a universal biological therapy for cancer will be found because of the nature of cancer. Despite the fact that all cancers are genetic diseases, there are still about 200 different cancers and they all have enough differences so that a one-size-fits-all biological therapy will not work. Cancer is a wily opponent, and many promising research ideas have reached a dead end. Others have succeeded, however, and are giving new hope to patients with previously untreatable cancer.

SUMMARY

Stem cell transplants kill cancer cells and support chemotherapy and radiation therapy treatments. Higher doses of chemotherapy drugs or radiation, which will normally kill a person's stem cells, can be given because the transplant replaces these cells. There are three types of stem cell transplants: autologous (patient's own stem cells), allogeneic (stems cells from a sibling), and syngeneic (stem cells from an identical twin). Biological therapies, which are the use of proteins to activate the immune system, have been developed to attack cancer cells directly without damaging normal cells in the process. Laboratories can produce naturally occurring cytokines such as interferon and interleukin for use in cancer therapy. Gene therapy is another newly developed treatment in which a virus is used to either replace defective genes with normal genes or to infect cancer cells.

8

COMPLEMENTARY AND ALTERNATIVE THERAPIES

KEY POINTS

♦ Complementary therapy means "complementing," or adding to, mainstream therapy. A patient will have mainstream therapy such as chemotherapy or radiation, and relieve cancer symptoms and side effects with other therapies such as meditation, yoga, diet, and herbs.

♦ Alternative therapy replaces mainstream therapy. A patient who takes this route chooses not to have chemotherapy, radiation, or surgery, and instead pursues other treatments.

♦ Alternative therapies are dangerous because none of them have been scientifically tested and proven successful.

Cheryl has been diagnosed with stage II bladder cancer, which means that the cancer has grown into the muscle layers of the bladder. She has begun chemotherapy to shrink the cancer and kill cancer cells that may have spread to other parts of the body. Cheryl will soon have surgery—a radical cystectomy that will remove the bladder, uterus, fallopian tubes, ovaries, and nearby lymph nodes. The surgery extends beyond the bladder to remove organs to which the cancer may have spread. The chemotherapy is causing nausea and vomiting, along with headaches. In addition to an-tinausea drugs and pain pills, Cheryl decides to try relaxation techniques. She lies down, closes her eyes, and concentrates on breathing in and out very slowly. After a few minutes she finds herself relaxed, and the side effects decrease noticeably. If the **pathology** laboratory results after the surgery show that the cancer has not spread to nearby organs, Cheryl will have a good chance of living many more years.

Dan has a very different mindset from Cheryl. He, too, was diagnosed with stage II bladder cancer, but he either did not believe that chemo-therapy and surgery would be effective, or did not want to put himself through the pain and discomfort of these treatments. He looked for other treatments by reading books and searching the Internet. Dan eventually decided to try several options. He eats a vegetarian diet, takes omega-3 fatty acid capsules, and drinks Essiac tea, made from a mixture of herbs.

Like Cheryl and Dan, about half of cancer patients turn to **comple-mentary therapy** or **alternative therapy**. Complementary therapy and alternative therapy are frequently confused with each other. A patient like Cheryl may choose to use a complementary therapy (complement means to complete) along with her mainstream cancer therapy—surgery, radiation therapy, chemotherapy, or biological therapy—to relieve the symptoms of cancer and the side effects of cancer therapy. Complementary therapies may include meditation, massage, yoga, diet, and dietary supplements such as vitamins, minerals, and herbs. Complementary therapies have been shown to improve the quality of life for some patients.

On the other hand, a patient like Dan may choose to use an alternative therapy *instead of* a mainstream cancer therapy. Some alternative therapies are identical to complementary therapies. Other alternative therapies involve chemicals or electrical devices. The difference between complementary therapies and alternative therapies is that patients turn to alternative therapies for a cancer cure and do not use mainstream cancer therapies.

COMPLEMENTARY THERAPIES

Complementary therapies may help with pain, nausea, stress, and depression. Many doctors are willing to help patients choose a complementary therapy if the patient thinks that he or she needs something beyond what the doctor can provide. Patients can meditate using several techniques, such as closing their eyes and concentrating on their breathing, or on a single word, until they reach a state of relaxation that can relieve pain and stress. Yoga can offer similar results. Many patients feel better if they take vitamins, minerals, and herbs. Peppermint tea, for example, can help with digestion.

Patients should check with their doctor, however, to make sure that a supplement doesn't interfere with their standard therapy. Some herbs can have a dangerous interaction with chemotherapy drugs. St. John's wort, for example, which some people use for depression, can reduce the blood level of certain chemotherapy drugs.

ALTERNATIVE THERAPIES

If you enter "cancer cure" into an Internet search engine, you will turn up more than 15 million hits. Many of these are the Web sites of mainstream medical establishments like the National Cancer Institute, the American

Cancer Society, hospitals, cancer centers, and medical journals. These Web sites offer information about diagnosing and treating cancer, and are straightforward about the nature of treatments and the predicted outcome—which may not be good for some cancers.

Other Web sites are definitely not part of mainstream medicine. They inform you of a "breakthrough" that "works with all cancers" and has supposedly "shocked the medical world." When you read on, you find that the Web sites often promote various "natural" substances, such as plant extracts, herbs, and minerals. People involved in promoting these cures usually don't have medical degrees, or have strange-sounding degrees from "colleges" that are not recognized as legitimate educational institutions. Cancer clinics in the United States and Mexico advertise themselves as the place to go for a cure that mainstream medicine cannot provide. Some Web sites use scientific-sounding language to talk about killing cancer cells with things like high oxygen levels and low acidity. Stories of people who cured their cancer are common. You can order books and videos that reveal the secrets of curing cancer without having to cope with doctors, hospitals, and painful and frightening procedures.

Many alternative therapies promote dietary supplements as cures for cancer. Dietary supplements are vitamins, minerals, and other substances that people take to supply nutrients that may be missing from the foods they eat. Essiac tea is a mixture of herbs used to make a tea that supporters claim "reduces or eliminates cancerous tumors." The plant aloe vera supposedly acts against a cancer's "abnormal cells." Various "metabolic" therapies use special diets, vitamins, minerals, and enzymes to cure cancer by removing "toxins"—poisonous substances—from the body. Although many dietary supplements are useful in maintaining good nutrition, there is no evidence that they cure cancer.

Proponents of various electromagnetic therapies claim to cure cancer by directing electromagnetic energy into the body. The Rife Machine supposedly emits radio waves that are the same frequency as those of bacteria that the proponents claim to cause cancer. The bacteria are destroyed. Proponents of BioResonance Tumor Therapy claim that their machine can detect electromagnetic oscillations—vibrations in electrical and magnetic fields—from cancer tumors and destroy them by "energizing the *p53* gene." Clinics in Mexico offer electromagnetic cancer therapy that is supposed to cure cancer by killing cancer cells. Despite the scientific-sounding theories, these, and other electromagnetic therapies, have no scientific basis. The machines cannot do what is stated in their advertisements.

Why are alternative therapies appealing to cancer patients? Mainstream cancer therapies cannot help all patients with cancer, so some turn to alternative therapies as a last resort. These patients may spend quite a bit of money and even travel out of the country to get treatments that are illegal in the United States. Other patients fear the side effects of mainstream therapy. Some see mainstream medicine as cold, impersonal technology, and find alternative therapies more in tune with their emotional needs. Also, as medicine has become more complex over the last century, there has been a reaction against modern medicine that shows itself in outright distrust and a search for simple and natural explanations for diseases and how to cure them. Alternative therapies give patients a simple explanation of why they have cancer—frequently based on "toxins"—and a seemingly logical way of treating it, allowing patients to feel that they understand the disease and are in control of their therapy.

All alternative therapies have one thing in common: they have never been put through the rigorous process of first studying them in animals and then moving on to clinical trials with patients (see Chapter 7). The lesson learned over the past century is that any new therapy must be thoroughly tested and reviewed to weed out things that simply don't work, despite supporters' claims.

Some of the alternative therapies are dangerous. The megadoses of vitamins prescribed can be toxic. The ingredients in herbs can vary considerably from one batch to another because of the age of the plant, the species, and where it was grown, making dosage uncertain and an overdose quite easy. The lesson is that just because something is natural doesn't mean that it is safe. The biggest danger is that when patients use an alternative therapy, they will not benefit from proven cancer therapies, or may delay using standard therapies until it is obvious that the alternative therapy has failed, and the cancer has already spread.

IS IT LEGAL?

Are there laws against making claims to cure cancer? The legal issue is complicated, and cancer patients are largely on their own in judging cancer "cures." Under FDA regulations a drug must be proven safe and effective through a "well-controlled investigation." No alternative therapies satisfy FDA drug regulations, and therefore they cannot claim to be drugs. Many substances that are claimed to cure cancer are covered under FDA food regulations, usually as dietary supplements.

FDA regulations for dietary supplements are weak compared to drug regulations. The FDA regulations are based on the Dietary Supplement Health and Education Act of 1994, which has been criticized as bowing to pressure from the dietary supplement industry and being too lenient on dietary supplements. The package labels on dietary supplements cannot claim to "treat, cure, or prevent any disease." Other, less specific, promises are permitted, however. Products may say they "boost the immune system" or "help cell membrane stability." No regulations prohibit claims for cancer cures made in books, radio and TV ads, and on the Internet as long as the cancer cures aren't being sold by those making the claims. These media are largely responsible for supporting the sales of dietary supplements and other cancer cures that are outside of mainstream medicine.

♦ APRICOTS, POLITICS, AND CANCER

Throughout his life, U.S. doctor Ernst T. Krebs Sr. developed formulas made from different substances and promoted them as cures for cancer and other diseases. He made one from apricot pits in the 1920s, but it proved too toxic. In the early 1950s he and his son Ernst T. Krebs Jr. refined a compound from apricot pits and claimed that it would kill cancer cells. They named the compound Laetrile, and it soon gained promoters. By the 1960s scientific studies had concluded that Laetrile had no effect on cancer, and in 1971, the FDA banned Laetrile from being shipped between states.

Despite these setbacks Laetrile became more and more popular with cancer patients, who frequently traveled to clinics in Mexico for treatment. By the end of the 1970s perhaps 70,000 Americans had been treated with Laetrile. Bowing to pressure from supporters, more than 20 states passed laws that allowed the sale of Laetrile. The pressure to legalize Laetrile increased to the point that, in 1977, Senator Edward Kennedy chaired a Senate hearing on Laetrile. The results were not good for Laetrile providers, whom Kennedy called "slick salesmen who would offer a false sense of hope" to cancer patients.

TESTING COMPLEMENTARY AND ALTERNATIVE THERAPIES

Supporters make exaggerated claims for alternative therapies, but that doesn't necessarily mean that all of them are worthless. After all some cancer treatments, such as paclitaxel from yew trees, come from natural sources. The difference between proponents of alternative therapies and scientists is that the proponents of alternative therapies do not conduct scientific studies to back up their claims. In a contro-

There was more bad news to come for Laetrile. In 1980 actor Steve McQueen was treated with Laetrile at a Mexican clinic and died soon after. That same year the National Cancer Institute began a clinical trial of Laetrile on 178 patients with advanced cancer. Within five months half the patients had either died or their tumors had grown larger. The study concluded that Laetrile was useless.

We know that Laetrile is really amygdalin, a compound discovered in 1830. Its supporters claim that it kills cancer cells by producing cyanide. That's true enough—serious illness and death from cyanide poisoning have occurred in cancer patients taking Laetrile. Today, after more than 50 years of controversy, Laetrile is still sold in the United States despite being illegal. The federal government does prosecute some cases. For years Jason Vale, president of Christian Brothers Contracting Corporation of New York, had promoted Laetrile heavily over the Internet and through "spam" e-mail. He was placed under court order in 2000 to stop promoting and selling Laetrile. He continued the sales in secret from the basement of his home, and in June 2004 was sentenced to 63 months in prison.

versial move Congress established the National Center for Complementary and Alternative Medicine (NCCAM) in 1998 to scientifically study complementary and alternative therapies in medical applications, including cancer.

The move to establish NCCAM was controversial. Many doctors and scientists feared that it made unscientific practices seem legitimate and created a special category of cancer therapies that do not have to undergo the rigorous testing that other therapies do. To them, it was a purely antiscientific, political action brought about by lobbyists for complementary and alternative therapies. Supporters of NCCAM said that some complementary and alternative therapies might prove useful, and the only way to find out is to subject them to scientific testing. The controversy made for a lively debate, which continues today.

Several complementary therapies are now being evaluated for their ability in providing comfort to cancer patients:

- **acupuncture** to relieve neck and shoulder pain following surgery for head or neck cancer

- ginger as a treatment for nausea and vomiting caused by chemotherapy

- massage for the treatment of cancer fatigue

The following alternative therapies are currently being evaluated to see if they will fight cancer:

- mistletoe extract combined with chemotherapy for the treatment of solid tumors

- shark cartilage to shrink or slow the growth of colorectal cancer or breast cancer cells

◆ noni, a plant extract used in Pacific islands, to fight tumor growth and cancer symptoms

So far, no alternative therapies have been found to be effective in fighting cancer.

BUYER BEWARE

Difficult as it may be, a cancer patient should ask commonsense questions when evaluating alternative therapies. A patient should keep in mind the following standards that a mainstream therapy must meet:

◆ the treatment was scientifically studied and the results reviewed by other scientists and doctors

◆ the treatment was shown to be more effective than no treatment at all

◆ the benefit must clearly outweigh the potential harm

An objective evaluation of an alternative therapy should go beyond examining the promises it makes. Many characteristics of alternative therapies point to fraud:

◆ The therapy claims to be a "miracle cure" with no side effects. Unlike mainstream therapies that have significant side effects, alternative therapies are claimed to be harmless to the patient while they work to destroy cancer.

◆ The therapy is based on a theory that has no scientific basis. Colon therapy involves removing toxins from the large intestine by flushing it out with enemas of water, herbal solutions, or coffee. There is no evidence that toxins accumulate in the large intestine. Electromagnetic therapy machines are based on ideas regarding killing cancer cells that have no basis in fact.

- ♦ The claims are based only on individual personal stories. Only successful stories are reported, so the cure rate appears to be 100 percent.

- ♦ No proof, such as a biopsy, is offered that the patients who were "cured" actually had cancer. A patient may be incorrectly "diagnosed" with cancer by a practitioner of an alternative therapy, who then provides a cure.

- ♦ The therapy is used along with a mainstream therapy, which makes it impossible to tell which one is really causing the improvement. The alternative therapy alone is given credit.

A cold, hard look at history can provide a perspective: alternative therapies that claim to cure cancer have risen and fallen for more than a century, and none of them has proven effective.

SUMMARY

Complementary and alternative therapies are distinctly different from each other. Complementary therapy means adding to, or complementing, mainstream therapy; alternative therapy means replacing mainstream therapy with a different treatment. Some patients have found that complementing their chemotherapy or radiation treatments with yoga, meditation, herbs, or certain diets helps them relax and eases pain. Alternative therapy is a risky road to take. There are many Web sites, books, and individuals promoting alternative cures for cancer that are outside of mainstream medicine. None of these "cures" have been proven to cure cancer.

9

LIVING WITH CANCER

KEY POINTS

- More than one million people of varying ages and backgrounds are diagnosed with cancer each year.

- Cancer patients and their families experience great stress. Developing a positive attitude and a sense of having at least some control can help a patient cope with cancer.

- Cancer itself, as well as cancer therapies, can cause pain, but 90 percent of patients can get relief through aggressive treatment of pain.

- Some patients respond to the diagnosis of cancer with positive action: starting cancer support groups or volunteering for clinical trials of new cancer treatments.

It's a good thing that Jeremy was sitting down when Dr. O'Brien said, "The biopsy shows that you have cancer." Jeremy was 25 years old, and had seen Dr. O'Brien because of swelling in his neck and a puzzling fever that came and went. After ruling out other causes, Dr. O'Brien sent Jeremy to a surgical oncologist, who performed a needle biopsy of several lymph nodes. The pathologist's diagnosis: Hodgkin's disease, a cancer of the lymph nodes.

Jeremy reacted with disbelief. He felt healthy, and his first thought was, "This can't be true. There must be a mistake." Over the next few days, as he met with oncologists to discuss radiation therapy and chemotherapy, Jeremy's emotions swung between fear and anger, helplessness and hope. By the time therapy began, he had reached a state of quiet determination to win his battle with cancer.

Like Jeremy, over a million people in the United States are diagnosed with cancer each year and begin a journey through cancer therapy and recovery that can take many months or even years. If all goes well, the cancer does not return, but patients and their families must live with uncertainty for many years.

LIFE GOES ON

Cancer patients experience great stress even with successful therapy, and they and their families must deal with many emotions, ranging from despair to confidence. A sense of having at least some control over the situation helps cancer patients cope with their emotions. They can do this by learning about the cancer, working with their medical team to make decisions, and forming an idea of what to expect during the course of treatment. Patients may lose their sense of independence while at the hospital and when first returning home, but they can gradually assume some of their own care and begin to do simple household chores. Maintaining proper nutrition and getting exercise will help restore energy.

Perhaps the most important thing a patient can do is to develop a positive attitude. Actions that help create a positive attitude include making plans for the future, communicating openly with family and friends, and joining a cancer support group. A support group is a group of cancer patients that meets regularly for discussions. It can be led by a social worker, nurse, or psychologist, or may operate without a health professional. A support group may include patients with different kinds of cancer or be limited to specific cancers, such as breast cancer or colon cancer. Taking part in support groups gives patients the opportunity to share their stories, hear other patients' stories, and gather information.

In addition to coping with the effects of cancer and cancer therapies, patients worry about how their illness will affect their family. They feel the need to focus on financial affairs and how their children will be cared for if they don't survive. Family routines may be disrupted by therapy. A spouse may feel overwhelmed by taking on new responsibilities, and children may be confused. The patient or spouse should tell the children about the illness, explaining its effects and the treatment, and reassure the children that their parent is getting good care. The best course is for all family members to make an extra effort to communicate openly and not let emotions build up.

Some friends, relatives, and coworkers may avoid the patient because they are very uncomfortable about the idea of dealing with cancer. "I just don't know what to say," is a common thought. They may be so afraid of cancer that they don't want to be reminded of the disease. Patients can make others feel more comfortable by explaining the particular cancer they have and being honest about how they are feeling.

DEALING WITH SIDE EFFECTS

Lisa had a hysterectomy, performed by Dr. Rodriguez, to treat endometrial cancer (see Chapter 4). The surgery went well and Lisa was able to go home five days after surgery, but she continued to have pain for several weeks. Dr. Rodriguez prescribed hydrocodone, which Lisa could take every six hours if she needed to. Lisa also had significant fatigue at first, and found herself becoming very tired when she tried to do routine household chores like washing dishes. She began to pay more attention to getting enough sleep, eating well, and drinking fluids.

Like Lisa, most cancer patients suffer pain and fatigue. The cancer itself can cause pain as it invades the tissues of the body and puts pressure on nerves and blocks organs. Cancer therapies can also cause pain. Aside from death, most cancer patients fear pain the most. The good news is that 90 percent of patients can get pain relief. Doctors and hospitals are quite aggressive now in relieving their patients' pain.

The key to controlling pain is for the patient to communicate honestly with their doctor or nurse. A patient may think that pain is a normal part of the treatment and may not want to complain. But bearing pain is unnecessary most of the time, and the patient should discuss pain honestly, describing the type of pain, its location, and its intensity. Aggressive pain management can provide relief that makes the patient more comfortable and able to resume normal activities.

Pain medications include several classes of drugs, the strongest being **opioids** such as morphine, hydrocodone, and methadone. Some patients are worried that taking opioids can lead to addiction, but this is very rare in cancer patients. A patient may have withdrawal symptoms like anxiety, sleeplessness, chills, and sweating when the medication is stopped, but these can be managed by slowly decreasing the dose.

Other pain relief measures include nerve stimulation with acupuncture and electrical impulses. Complementary therapies such as relaxation, meditation, and yoga can also help to manage pain.

Fatigue is the most common side effect of cancer and cancer therapies. Patients vary greatly in experiencing fatigue, with their symptoms ranging from mild tiredness to total exhaustion. "I can't even put one foot in front of the other," a patient might think. Aside from the cancer itself and cancer therapies, fatigue can be caused by anemia, pain, stress, lack of sleep, and depression. As with pain, the first step in dealing with fatigue is for the patient to communicate honestly with the doctor or nurse. Patients can help manage fatigue by planning their time to conserve energy, exercising daily, eating well, drinking enough fluids, and establishing a regular sleep pattern.

A dietician can help select proper foods and the amounts to eat to get the calories the patient needs to preserve muscle mass, restore energy, and minimize side effects like nausea and vomiting caused by chemotherapy (see Chapter 6). In some cases, cancer therapies have temporary or permanent side effects that make proper nutrition difficult, such as a decrease in digestive system function, difficulty in swallowing, and a painful mouth and throat. The choice of foods (along with liquefying them) can help, in addition to liquid nutritional supplements. If food cannot be taken by mouth, a feeding tube is run into the stomach through the nose or through an incision in the abdomen.

BODY IMAGE

Elizabeth was diagnosed with breast cancer when she was 36 years old. Because the tumor had spread through much of her breast, surgeons performed a mastectomy to remove the entire breast. Elizabeth decided

◆ PATIENTS TALK ABOUT LIVING WITH CANCER

Dr. Jimmie C. Holland is a psychiatrist who works with cancer patients at Memorial Sloan-Kettering Cancer Center in New York. In her book *The Human Side of Cancer* (co-authored with Sheldon Lewis), many patients share their thoughts on how they live with their disease. Some of the thoughts are unexpected:

"I feel sometimes as if I'm caught in a gigantic bunch of moving gears. I panic for a minute . . . then take a deep breath and realize things aren't so bad. I'm actually coping well with a lot of stuff and the panicky feelings get back under control."

"For me, knowing that I was seriously ill opened doors and opportunities that have truly enriched my life. It is through cancer that I have rediscovered my love of painting and refocused my energies to help others. Both have given me tremendous strength and satisfaction."

"I would not have taken time to discover who I am and what life is about if I hadn't developed cancer."

"My friend had to have a breast biopsy. She was scared to death and needed a lot of support and asked me to go with her. When

not to have breast reconstruction surgery, and has a scar across her chest where her breast once was. Besides dying from cancer, what Elizabeth feared most was that she wouldn't feel like the same person after the

the procedure was over and the biopsy was negative and she was fine, she started to lecture me on how I have to be strong to cope with my lung cancer treatment. I wanted to hit her."

"At first, groups turned me off. I didn't like the idea of having to listen to other people's symptoms. If they were sicker than I, that would start me worrying about myself; if they were not as sick, that would make me jealous. But it actually turned out that we were all in the same leaky boat. We could understand what each other felt."

"My reactions, since my lung cancer came back, are like a roller-coaster ride. One day, I go shopping like crazy and buy new clothes and plan a thousand things to do. The next day, panic sets in, and I start cleaning out my closets and giving everything away."

"We all have to die sometime. I just happen to know a little more about how and when mine will be. It gives you time to plan and take care of things."

Source: Jimmie C. Holland, M.D. and Sheldon Lewis, *The Human Side of Cancer: Living with Hope, Coping with Uncertainty.* 2000, Reprinted by permission of HarperCollins Publishers.

surgery. She was right. Although she is married to a supportive husband and has two children, she nevertheless lost her sense of being a woman. She would not allow her husband to see her scar for many months, and had a difficult time accepting her new body. "I'm ugly. I'm not whole," she thought. By talking with her husband and her friends, she gradually began to feel more at ease and has now resumed her normal activities. She has even become comfortable enough with herself to make jokes about missing a breast.

Like Elizabeth, almost all people have an image of their bodies, which is closely tied to a sense of who they are and to their self-esteem. Cancer therapy can radically change a patient's body, and, therefore, can have a tremendous psychological effect. The loss of a breast may make a woman feel unattractive and even like she isn't a woman anymore. The loss of a testicle may be similarly devastating to a man. Having to excrete body wastes through a stoma into a bag can seem like a terrible humiliation.

Patients need to make a conscious effort to adjust to their new body and accept the changes that cancer has caused. The first step is for patients to look at the changes and become accustomed to them. This is not easy and takes time. Patients should also work on being able to show their body to doctors and nurses and to their spouse. Whether or not the change in the body is visible to others, it is important for the patient to become accustomed to going out in public and not to remain isolated at home. Wigs and clothing can hide the effects of cancer and let the patient feel more comfortable about being seen.

WHEN CANCER RETURNS

Louis was diagnosed two years ago with stomach cancer. The cancer was in the lower part of the stomach, and had spread to three nearby lymph nodes. Louis had surgery to remove most of his stomach and all nearby lymph nodes, followed by chemotherapy with fluorouracil.

Louis realized that his long-term survival was uncertain—the surgeon told him that the five-year survival rate was about 60 percent. After recovering and feeling well for more than a year, he began to lose weight and found himself not eating as much as usual. His doctor ordered some tests, and ultrasound imaging revealed a tumor in Louis's liver. Further tests showed several small tumors in his lungs as well. Louis's stomach cancer had metastasized to these organs. Surgery would not help. After the shock of realizing that he might not have long to live, Louis considered two options. One was palliative chemotherapy to slow down the growth of the tumors and make him feel more comfortable. Instead, Louis thought, "What do I have to lose?" and decided on the second option: participation in a clinical trial to test a new chemotherapy drug (see Chapter 7). The chance that the new drug would cure his advanced cancer was a long shot, but Louis wanted to help future cancer patients.

Although cancer therapy permanently gets rid of cancer in about half of patients, the rest experience additional cancer that develops months or years after the initial therapy. For some patients, like Louis, cancer cells entered the blood or lymph nodes and spread to other organs before therapy began. For other patients, the cancer recurs at or near the original site. Facing a recurrence can be more difficult for the patient than the original diagnosis. The failure of the initial cancer therapy may cause a loss of hope, and a patient may barely be able to think about going through another round of therapy.

For some patients, the cancer advances, and eventually therapy is not advised because the cancer is not responding and the therapy's side effects are severely affecting the patient's quality of life. The focus shifts from attempting to cure the cancer to providing psychological comfort and relief from pain. Patients and their families need to decide whether the patients will live out their remaining days in a hospital, at home, or in a hospice—a place designed to care for the terminally ill. Near the end of life, the patient will sleep more, eat less, and become weaker and confused. Signs that death is approaching include changes in breathing and heart rate, loss of sensation and reflexes, and going into a coma.

CANCER AND THE HUMAN SPIRIT

Whether or not patients survive their battle with cancer, their lives are changed the minute they hear the words, "You have cancer." They now face their greatest challenge. Some patients turn this tragedy into a positive event, going so far as to say that having cancer made them realize what is important in life and transformed them into better people. In his book, *It's Not About the Bike: My Journey Back to Life*, champion bicycle racer Lance Armstrong (see Chapter 1) said, "The truth is, if you asked me to choose between winning the Tour de France and cancer, I would choose cancer. Odd as it sounds, I would rather have the title of cancer survivor than winner of the Tour, because of what it has done for me as a human being, a husband, a son, and a father."

A few cancer patients have faced the challenge head-on by starting national cancer support groups. Others show their spunk by shocking friends with an old joke: "I don't have to worry about getting cancer anymore—I've got it." Despite the trauma of having cancer, modern medicine has cured some cancer patients and given additional years of life to others. Many people use this gift of time to the fullest by making their lives more meaningful for themselves and their family and friends.

SUMMARY

Cancer and cancer therapies can cause pain. Patients who communicate openly with doctors about their pain can get relief with medications as well as complementary therapies like yoga, meditation, and acupuncture. Dealing with cancer emotionally is as important as dealing with it physically. Fear, anger, stress, hopelessness, and other feelings arise when patients are faced with cancer. Sharing their feelings with family, friends, doctors, and in professional support groups can help ease a patient's sense of being alone and provide alternative perspectives on the disease. If the cancer is not treatable, patients can choose to have palliative treatment and live out their remaining days in the comfort of their own homes. The diagnosis of cancer is not always necessarily a death sentence. For many people, it is an experience that causes them to evaluate their priorities and live a more meaningful life.

GLOSSARY

◆

acupuncture   A procedure that originated in China in which specific points on the body are pierced with thin needles to relieve pain or bring about some other desired effect

acute lymphocytic leukemia   A type of leukemia in which immature white blood cells are produced in massive numbers by the bone marrow and crowd out normal cells. It can spread to the bloodstream and organs.

alkylating agent   A chemical compound that adds an alkyl group to a biological molecule, most commonly DNA

alkyl group   A group of carbon and hydrogen atoms connected to one another by single chemical bonds

alternative therapy   A therapy that a patient turns to instead of mainstream medicine. Alternative therapies have not been scientifically proven to be safe or effective.

anaphylaxis   A severe and sometimes fatal reaction caused by being exposed to an antigen more than once

anemia   A decrease in the blood's ability to carry oxygen, caused by a low number of red blood cells or a decrease in hemoglobin molecules in the red blood cells

anesthesia   The loss of the sensation of pain brought about by a drug (an anesthetic). Anesthesia may affect part of the body (local or regional anesthesia) or cause unconsciousness (general anesthesia).

anesthesiologist   A doctor who administers an anesthetic

anesthetic   A drug that causes a loss of the sensation of pain

angiogenesis   The formation of new blood vessels

132

antiangiogenesis drug   A drug that blocks the formation of blood vessels (angiogenesis) in tumors so that they stop growing

antibiotic   A drug that can kill bacteria and other harmful microorganisms

antibodies   Proteins of the immune system that attack bacteria, viruses, and other foreign invaders. An antibody is specific to one antigen, and the body produces thousands of different antibodies to attack different invaders.

antigen   The protein or carbohydrate molecules on the surface of a bacteria, virus, or other invader that cause the body to produce an antibody to attack and destroy the invader

antimetabolite   A drug that is similar to a metabolite (an essential chemical) and therefore interferes with the cellular processes involving the metabolite

antiseptic   A substance that prevents infection or disease by inhibiting the growth of microorganisms

antitumor antibiotic   A drug that binds to DNA and prevents RNA from being produced. The cancer cell dies because key proteins can no longer be produced.

apoptosis   The automatic death of an unwanted or damaged cell

B cell   A type of lymphocyte that produces an antibody when stimulated by an antigen, which are the molecules on the surface of a foreign invader. The antibody attaches itself to the antigen and kills the foreign invader or marks it for destruction by other cells of the immune system.

benign   Referring to a tumor that does not invade normal tissue

bilirubin   A waste product from the breakdown of red blood cells that is removed from blood by the liver

biopsy   The removal of tissue for examination under a microscope and other tests

blood cell count   The measure of the amount of each type of blood cell in a blood sample, including white blood cells, red blood cells, and platelets. A high or low count may indicate disease.

bone marrow   The soft, sponge-like tissue in the center of bones that produces red and white blood cells

bronchoscope   A flexible fiber-optic tube that is inserted through the mouth or nose to examine the lungs

carcinogen   A substance or other agent that causes cancer

carcinoma   A cancer that occurs in the tissues that line the inside and outside of organs (epithelium). It occurs in the skin, breast, lung, colon, cervix, stomach, and other organs.

catheter   A plastic tube that is inserted into the body (usually a blood vessel or the urethra) to add or drain fluids

cerebrospinal fluid   The fluid that circulates through the brain and spinal cord

cervix   The lower part of the uterus that joins the vagina

chemotherapy   Using drugs to destroy cancer cells

chromosome   A thin strand in the nucleus of a cell made of DNA and proteins

clinical trial   A research study with human subjects that evaluates new drugs and other therapies to see if they are safe and effective

colon   Also called the large intestine. The colon absorbs water from waste material before it is expelled through the rectum and out the anus.

colonoscope   A long, flexible endoscope used to examine the colon

colostomy   An operation in which the lower part of the colon is removed. The remainder of the colon is attached to a new opening (a stoma) in the abdomen through which body waste will be excreted.

complementary therapy   A treatment that a patient uses in addition to mainstream medicine to help relieve pain, stress, and other unpleasant symptoms of disease or side effects of therapy

computerized tomography   Using a computer-controlled X-ray machine to make a three-dimensional image of the interior of the body

creatinine   A breakdown product from muscle tissues. It is filtered out of the blood by the kidneys.

cryosurgery   A procedure that kills diseased tissue or cancer cells using extreme cold

cyst   An abnormal sac filled with a fluid or soft material

cytokine   A protein released by an immune system cell. Cytokines regulate communication between different parts of the immune system.

cytology   The study of the structure of cells

cystoscope   A flexible fiber-optic tube that is inserted through the urethra and used to observe the urinary tract and bladder

diabetes   The word commonly refers to insulin-dependent diabetes, a serious disease caused by the body not producing enough insulin, a hormone that metabolizes carbohydrates

differentiate   When an immature cell develops into a specialized cell with a specific function in the body

DNA   Abbreviation for deoxyribonucleic acid. DNA is the double-stranded molecule in the nucleus of all cells that contains genetic information.

electrocardiogram   A test that measures the electrical activity of the heart to detect abnormalities

electromagnetic radiation   The radiation made of electric and magnetic fields. All forms of electromagnetic radiation move at the speed of light and differ only in their wavelength. They include visible, ultraviolet, and infrared light; X-rays, microwaves, and radar; and communication radiation for television, radio, and cell phones.

electron   A negatively charged subatomic particle that orbits an atom's nucleus

endometrium   The membrane that lines the uterus

endoscopy   Using a narrow, flexible fiber-optic tube (an endoscope) that transmits an image to examine certain parts of the interior of the body, such as the colon, stomach, and bladder

endotracheal tube   A tube inserted through the mouth or nose down the trachea (windpipe) to the entrance of the lungs to keep the airway open

enzyme   A protein that speeds up a specific chemical reaction to millions of times faster than it would normally occur

epithelium   A layer of cells that lines the internal and external surfaces of the body

esophagus   The muscular tube that pushes food from the mouth to the stomach

estrogen   One of a group of hormones secreted mainly by the ovaries that regulate the female reproductive system and develop female secondary sex characteristics such as breasts

five-year survival rate   The percentage of patients who live at least five years after cancer is diagnosed

gene A unit of heredity that consists of a long section of DNA

gynecologist A doctor who specializes in disorders of the female reproductive organs

hematopoietic stem cell Stem cells in the bone marrow that can develop into several types of blood cells

hepatitis An inflammation of the liver caused by viruses, alcohol, chemicals, and other agents

hormone A chemical messenger produced by a gland that circulates throughout the body. Different hormones have widely different functions, including the promotion of growth and development and the regulation of organs.

hysterectomy The surgical removal of the uterus

immune system The system of organs and cells that recognizes and attacks foreign organisms and substances

intravenous Literally means "into" a vein, referring to medicine or nutrients introduced through a needle or catheter

isotope A chemical element can have atoms with different atomic weights, which nevertheless have the same chemical properties. The atoms of each atomic weight are called an isotope: carbon-12, carbon-13, and carbon-14, for example, are three isotopes of carbon.

laparotomy A surgical incision through the abdomen

larynx A 2-inch (5-cm) organ in the neck at the top of the windpipe that contains the vocal cords, also called the voice box

lesion A wound or an abnormal change in tissue

leukemia A cancer of the bone marrow cells that produce blood cells. Leukemia is marked by a large number of abnormal white blood cells.

ligament   A band of strong tissue that connects bones to other bones and to cartilage, and supports some internal organs

liposomal therapy   Chemotherapy drugs that are placed inside liposomes (artificial fat globules). Liposomes penetrate cancer cells more readily than they do normal cells, and thus reduce side effects of chemotherapy.

lymphatic system   The system of lymph nodes, organs, and thin tubes that produce lymph fluid and transport it throughout the body. The lymphatic system contains white blood cells and is part of the immune system.

lymph node   A small capsule containing white blood cells that is part of the immune system. It filters out and destroys bacteria, viruses, and toxins that are in the lymph fluid.

lymphocyte   A type of white blood cell that includes B cells and T cells, making up about 25 percent of a person's white blood cells

lymphoma   A cancer of the lymph nodes, the small capsules that are part of the immune system

magnetic resonance imaging (MRI)   A process that uses a machine to produce strong magnetic fields and radio waves to create an image of the interior of the body

malignant   Referring to a tumor that invades normal tissue and may metastasize to distant parts of the body

mammogram   An X-ray procedure that produces an image of the breast

margin   The tissue surrounding a cancer tumor

mastectomy   The removal of all or part of a breast

medical physicist   A scientist who specializes in applying physics to medicine, generally in the fields of medical imaging and radiation therapy

melanoma   A dark tumor that occurs on the skin and frequently metastasizes to other parts of the body

metabolic tests   Tests to determine whether chemical processes in the body are normal

metabolism   The chemical processes occurring in a cell and in the entire organism that are necessary for life

metastasize   To spread to other parts of the body through the blood or lymphatic system

mitotic inhibitor   A drug that stops the division of a cell nucleus (mitosis)

mononucleosis   An infectious disease, usually not serious, caused by the Epstein-Barr virus. Symptoms include fever, swollen lymph nodes, and sore throat.

mutation   A change in the DNA of a gene in a cell that results in a new trait. Mutations can be passed on when the cell divides.

myeloma   A cancer of the bone marrow cells that produce antibodies

natural killer cell   A type of lymphocyte that attacks cells infected with viruses

nucleus   The nucleus of a cell is the central part that contains DNA and acts as the cell's control center. The nucleus of an atom is the central part that contains protons and neutrons.

oncogene   A mutated gene that can cause a cell to be transformed into a cancer cell

oncologist   A doctor who specializes in treating cancer

opioid   A drug such as morphine or oxycodone that acts on the central nervous system to relieve pain

organic compound   A natural or man-made compound that contains carbon and hydrogen, and usually other elements such as oxygen and nitrogen

organism   Any form of life such as a plant, animal, or bacterium

ovary   One of two almond-size glands that are found on either side of the uterus

palliation   Relieving pain or other discomfort without trying to cure the disease

pathologist   A doctor who specializes in diagnosing disease

pathology   The study of the nature of diseases, their causes, and how they develop

pediatric   Referring to the medical care of infants and children

phagocyte   A white blood cell that engulfs and ingests foreign invaders such as bacteria

platelet   A blood cell that helps to clot the blood to stop bleeding

polyp   An abnormal growth projecting from the surface of a mucous membrane such as the membrane in the colon, nose, or uterus

positron emission tomography (**PET**)   A process that creates an image of a cancer by recording the radiation emitted by radioactive isotopes that have been absorbed by the cancer cells

prostate   A walnut-sized gland below the bladder in males that supplies fluid to semen, the sperm-containing secretion

prostatectomy   The surgical removal of all or part of the prostate gland

protein   A large biological molecule composed of smaller units called amino acids. Proteins include enzymes, hormones, antibodies, and other molecules that are necessary for biological processes.

radioactive element   An element that can emit particles or electromagnetic radiation from its nucleus

rectum   The last part of the colon. Body waste is stored in the rectum before being pushed out of the anus.

remission When a cancer disappears or at least shrinks in size and symptoms disappear

repair enzyme An enzyme that repairs damaged DNA

right atrial chamber One of four chambers in the heart. It pumps oxygen-depleted blood arriving from the body into the right ventricle chamber, from which the blood is pumped into the lungs to receive oxygen.

RNA Abbreviation for ribonucleic acid. RNA is similar to a single strand of DNA, and transfers information from the DNA in the nucleus out into the cell to make proteins.

sarcoma A cancer of the connective or supportive tissue in bones, tendons, muscle, and fat

squamous cells Flattened cells that line an epithelium. Various epithelia cover the internal and external surfaces of the body.

stem cell An undeveloped cell that can develop into a specialized cell such as a white blood cell. A particular type of stem cell from an adult is limited to developing into a certain type of cell. A stem cell from an embryo can develop into any type of cell in the body.

stoma An artificial opening created by surgery through which body waste is excreted

T cell A type of lymphocyte that recognizes foreign invaders and attacks them, and also releases proteins called cytokines that call other immune cells into action

telomerase An enzyme that can add DNA to the telomeres of chromosomes. Cells can then divide over and over without dying, a characteristic of cancer.

telomere The section of DNA at the tip of a chromosome

testicle   One of a pair of male sex organs in the scrotum that produce sperm

testosterone   The male sex hormone that causes the development of the male reproductive organs and male secondary sex characteristics such as facial hair and muscular development

thyroid gland   A gland in the neck that produces hormones necessary for growth and metabolism

tumor   An abnormal growth of tissue caused by uncontrolled cell division

tumor marker   A substance released by cancer cells. Different tumor markers indicate different types of cancer.

tumor suppressor gene   A gene that controls cell division. If a tumor suppressor gene is mutated and can't function, a cell can become cancerous and grow and divide without limit.

ultrasound   The use of sound waves to make an image of the interior of the body

urethra   The tube through which urine drains from the bladder

uterus   A hollow muscular organ in which a fertilized egg develops into a fetus

virus   A tiny, infectious particle consisting of a core of DNA or RNA and a protein coat. Viruses cannot reproduce themselves unless they are in an animal or plant cell.

FURTHER RESOURCES

◆

Bibliography

American Cancer Society. *American Cancer Society's Guide to Complementary and Alternative Cancer Methods.* Atlanta, Ga.: American Cancer Society, 2000.

Armstrong, Lance, with Sally Jenkins. *It's Not About the Bike: My Journey Back to Life.* New York: G. P. Putnam's Sons, 2000.

Dollinger, Malin, Ernest H. Rosenbaum, Margaret Tempero, and Sean J. Mulvihill. *Everyone's Guide to Cancer Therapy: How Cancer Is Diagnosed, Treated, and Managed Day to Day*, 4th ed. Kansas City, Mo.: Andrews McMeel, 2002.

Eyre, Harmon J., Dianne Partie Lange, and Lois B. Morris. *Informed Decisions: The Complete Book of Cancer Diagnosis, Treatment, and Recovery*, 2nd ed. Atlanta, Ga.: American Cancer Society, 2002.

Ezzell, Carol. "Magic Bullets Fly Again." *Scientific American* 285 (October 2001): 34–41.

Gibbs, W. Wayt. "Untangling the Roots of Cancer." *Scientific American* 289 (July 2003): 56–65.

Holland, Jimmie C., and Sheldon Lewis. *The Human Side of Cancer: Living with Hope, Coping with Uncertainty.* New York: HarperCollins, 2000.

Kufe, Donald, ed. *Cancer Medicine.* Hamilton, Ontario: B. C. Decker, 2003.

Morra, Marion, and Eve Potts. *Choices: The Most Complete Sourcebook for Cancer Information*, 4th ed. New York: HarperCollins, 2003.

Panno, Joseph. *Cancer: The Role of Genes, Lifestyle, and Environment.* New York: Facts On File, 2005.

Rubin, Philip. *Clinical Oncology: A Multidisciplinary Approach for Physicians and Students*, 8th ed. Philadelphia: W. B. Saunders, 2001.

Schimmel, Selma R., with Barry Fox. *Cancer Talk: Voices of Hope and Endurance from "The Group Room," the World's Largest Cancer Support Group.* New York: Broadway Books, 1999.

Teeley, Peter, and Philip Bashe. *The Complete Cancer Survival Guide.* New York: Doubleday, 2000.

Zakarian, Beverly. *The Activist Cancer Patient: How to Take Charge of Your Treatment.* New York: John Wiley & Sons, 1996.

Web Sites

Abramson Cancer Center of the University of Pennsylvania
http://www.oncolink.org
> "A Chemotherapy Primer: Why? What? and How?" by Julia Draznin Maltzman.

American Cancer Society
http://www.cancer.org
> *Articles*: "Cancer Facts and Figures 2005"; "Oncogenes and Tumor Suppressor Genes"; "Testing Biopsy and Cytology Specimens for Cancer"; "Cancer Prevention & Early Detection Facts and Figures 2005"; "Surgery"; "Detailed Guide: Laryngeal and Hypopharyngeal Cancer"; "Detailed Guide: Endometrial Cancer"; "Detailed Guide: Leukemia—Acute Lymphocytic"; "Chemotherapy Principles."

American Society of Clinical Oncology
http://www.plwc.org
> *Articles*: "Coping;" "People Living With Cancer."

Chemical & Engineering News
http://pubs.acs.org/cen/coverstory/83/8325/8325taxol.html
> *Article*: "Taxol."

Dana-Farber Cancer Institute
http://www.dana-farber.org/abo/history/who
> *Article*: "Who Was Sidney Farber?"

Emory University

http://www.cancerquest.org

> *Articles*: "Cancer Biology," "Detection and Treatment."

Joseph Lister and Antiseptic Surgery

http://web.ukonline.co.uk/b.gardner/Lister.html

Lance Armstrong Foundation

http://www.livestrong.org

> *Article*: "Survivorship Stories."

Massachusetts General Hospital and Harvard University

http://neurosurgery.mgh.harvard.edu/History/ether1.htm

> *Article*: "We Have Conquered Pain. A Celebration of Ether 1846–1996."

National Cancer Institute

http://www.cancer.gov

> *Articles*: "Cancer and the Environment"; "Cancer Causes and Risk Factors"; "Cancer Imaging"; "Cancer Screening Overview"; "Radiation Therapy for Cancer: Questions and Answers"; "Bone Marrow Transplantation and Peripheral Blood Stem Cell Transplantation: Questions and Answers"; "Biological Therapies for Cancer: Questions and Answers"; "Complementary and Alternative Medicine"; "Staging: Questions and Answers."

National Institutes of Health

http://rex.nci.nih.gov/behindthenews/cioc/ciochome.htm

> *Article*: "Closing In On Cancer: Solving a 5000-Year-Old Mystery."

Public Health Institute Breast Cancer Answers

http://www.canceranswers.org

University of Dayton Chronology Project

http://www.udayton.edu/~hume/Lister/lister.htm

> *Article*: "The Father of Modern Surgery."

Yale-New Haven Teachers Institute

http://www.yale.edu/ynhti/curriculum/units/1983/7/83.07.01.x.html

> *Article*: "An Historical Overview of the Discovery of the X-Ray," by Joyce Calarco.

INDEX

◆

3 2186 00174 6147

Fossil Ridge Public Library District
Braidwood, IL 60408

ABOUT THE AUTHOR

◆

LYMAN LYONS grew up in Cajun country in southern Louisiana, and was interested in biology as a young boy. He spent much of his free time fishing and collecting snakes, lizards, and turtles in the subtropical swamps and bayous. His interest turned to physical science in high school, and he earned a B.S. in chemistry from the University of Louisiana–Lafayette and an M.A. in the history of science from the University of Wisconsin. Lyman did research in chemistry and in science education at the University of Wisconsin. He taught high school science and mathematics in Seattle, Washington, and wrote seminars and handbooks on mathematics teaching. He is now a freelance editor and writer living with his wife in McFarland, Wisconsin.